Acknowledgments

I wish to thank the people who again and again have been there for me, in good times and hard, who have contributed to my understanding and who have stood by me. I would like to thank Karen Silverman for her being there and for her information and channeling. Her input on abductions and the Greys for this book was needed and particularly helpful. I thank Corinne Nichols for her always pertinent and awesome grasp of planetary changes and Earth energies. She always knows just what to do and where to look next. Thanks also to Connie Repoli for her healing work on me in some of the hardest times of my life. I thank Missy Tibbs for everyday support, unfailing calm, and total common sense, and Leah Jeansdaughter for showing me Archangel Michael's Sword and Chalice.

Every day I give thanks for Elaine Goldman Gill, for her friendship and her support in publishing my books. I appreciate her deeply for trusting me in what I do, strange as what I do and write about usually is. I also thank all the people of The Crossing Press for making, publishing, and marketing my books in the very best quality possible. They are consistently wonderful and I deeply thank them all.

*for Archangel Michael, Protector of the Light,
and for Brede the Light Herself*

DIANE STEIN'S

RELIANCE
ON
THE
LIGHT

PSYCHIC PROTECTION
with the LORDS OF KARMA
and the GODDESS

THE CROSSING PRESS
BERKELEY, CALIFORNIA

The Crossing Press
www.crossingpress.com

A division of Ten Speed Press
P.O. Box 7123
Berkeley, California 94707
www.tenspeed.com

Library of Congress Cataloging-in-Publication Data

Stein, Diane, 1948-
    Reliance on the Light : psychic protection with the Lords of Karma and the Goddess / Diane Stein.
        p. cm.
      ISBN 1-58091-090-4 (pbk.)
      1. Self-defense--Psychic aspects I. Title.

    BF1045.S46 S84 2001
    133.8--dc21

                                                    2001028097

Cover design by Victoria May
Cover art by Jody Hewgill
Interior design by Nathan Walker

First printing, 2001
Printed in the United States of America

                2 3 4 5 6 7 8 9 10—07 06 05 04 03

Contents

If I can give in these pages the knowledge which protects, I shall have fulfilled my purpose.

—Dion Fortune, Psychic Self-Defense

1

INTRODUCTION

As always, I ask for the help and protection of the Light in the writing of this book. The words come from Brede, my Goddess, and the protection and help from a variety of discarnate sources. They come from the Lords of Karma, Archangels Ashtar and Michael, Divine Director, Ascended Master El Morya, and the Goddesses in their many names. They come from many sources and many forces of the Light, originating on Earth and on other planets. I define Light as meaning the radiant energy of life and goodness, as information and understanding, and as the radiant force of soul evolution. Light radiates and permeates, it streams forth over, around, under, and through our Be-ings and the Be-ing of all life. It permeates the Earth. Light is life. Light is what is good.

This is not to say that darkness is evil. The positive dark, as part of the radiant energy of life, is Light as well. All life emerges from the dark, from the Void, from the pregnant womb of creation that is located in the planetary Mind Grid. Earth's creation Goddess, Nada, whose name in Spanish means "nothing," is the dark void and pregnant womb from which all life descends. All that is manifest—the Light, the Nonvoid—comes from Nada's Void and positive darkness. Goodness is a balance of Light and the positive dark, of Void and Nonvoid (nonmanifest and manifest Be-ing). After day comes night and after the bright Full Moon comes the dark of the New Moon. Dark and Light follow each other. Both are life and both are Light.

Goodness, however, is not the whole story. While the Earth and all life were created by Nada, the Great Mother, in purity and perfection, that perfection has been repeatedly compromised. Our purity and the Earth's was damaged at the beginning of creation by an attempted hostile takeover of the planetary Mind Grid. This Mind Grid of the Earth is the Void's "computer" through which all life is formed. Earth has been the site of intergalactic warfare since its creation, and all Earth life and Earth Light has been harmed by it. The purity of life, Light, the positive darkness, and the planet has been embattled, damaged, harmed, and all but lost, but Light will always ultimately prevail.

In living on the Earth, we can no longer acknowledge just the existence of Light. We must also recognize and heal the positive darkness of the Earth and of ourselves, our creation that has been so badly damaged through the co-opting of the planet. Though it is even more difficult, we must acknowledge the existence of the other side—that there is the negative dark, and that there is evil in the world. We have lost our perfection and the Earth's and it is time to regain the full force and purity of our Light and of our goodness. Though it is said that Light and dark must co-exist, that neither exists without the other, this is only true of the positive dark, of the Void and Nonvoid. The negative dark—evil in the world—is not part of our creational plan and it is not meant to exist at all. But evil does exist, and our lives come up against it daily.

It seems a feature of the New Age and Women's Spirituality, Goddess Spirituality, and Wicca that the negative dark is refused and not acknowledged. Goddess and Women's Spirituality and

Wicca do recognize the Light and the positive dark only, while the New Age movement recognizes only the Light and denies darkness, the positive and negative both. Buddhism describes all living as unremitting suffering, and the Christian Right sees evil everywhere without discovering that Light exists at all. Life on Earth, human and otherwise, was created in a balanced perfection of Light and positive darkness but has been damaged and harmed by creational evil. The Source of All Evil was the attack on planetary creation, Nada, and the planetary Mind Grid by Be-ings of other planets attempting to claim ownership of Earth. All that lives carries harm by evil. All that lives was created in goodness, and is basically and intrinsically good. We are not evil and we have the ability to regain our purity.

In my years of work with women, I have often wondered that so many people deny that evil exists. When I talk about the negative dark, or how to heal and protect ourselves from it, I receive incredulous and often negative reactions. "If you refuse its existence it can't hurt you," I'm told. Or, "If you think about that stuff you give it power." "Ignore it and it goes away," they say. And, "What's wrong with you that you're talking about needing protection?" The fact is that, like a child hiding in a closet from a fire, the fire won't go away by ignoring or refusing to acknowledge its existence. What you refuse to recognize and deal with can indeed hurt you.

Perhaps many women deny the existence of evil in the world simply because it is too scary. If they admit it exists they are also admitting that there is something to fear. Or they'll have to do something about what they fear. So, rather than fear it, they deny it. I have had women challenge me on the subject of negative interference—evil hampering their freedom and their lives—only to change their minds after a meditation on protection from or clearing of evil shows them that something is indeed there. A number of methods of protection, clearing, and healing from evil and negative interference can be used to deal with evil. Instead of hiding from the fire, put it out. To understand that there is evil in the world, just watch or listen to the daily news. The media presents us with a continual litany of wrongs committed and received on the planet, in our own and other countries, in our home towns. There is so much male violence (and most violence is male), that we lose count of the losses and the deaths. We hear of so many wars, shootings, crimes, horrors, and disasters that we become hardened, and almost can't accept them as real anymore. We watch and hear of so much pain we can't let it into our consciousness fully or the pain would paralyze our daily lives.

When enough people have ended the interference of evil in their own lives, we will reach a critical mass that will end evil on Earth forever. As each aspect of negative darkness is removed from us, our Light vibration rises. When enough Light vibrations are raised, the planet is raised. Each Be-ing's nonphysical energy system contains an individual Mind Grid, each person's creational computer. All individual Mind Grids are part of the planetary Mind Grid. We create with our minds, bringing thought (the Void) into manifestation (the Nonvoid). Thought is Light, created from the positive darkness. By clearing and healing our individual thought computers, our Mind Grids, we clear and heal the Earth's Mind Grid. By changing our thinking, we heal ourselves, the Earth, and the Great Goddess. Eventually we will change the daily news.

The purpose of this book is to help you understand negative interference, what it is and how it operates, and to remove it from your energy, your Mind Grid. Each change from negative to positive, from interference to the Light, increases your total energy vibration. Each change creates a way for healing and freedom.

You should not fear evil. You should not deny it. You should not let it operate in your life and do harm. By changing the operation of your Mind Grid so that the negative darkness cannot function there, you allow for the radiance of the Light to fill and heal your energy system and your life. We are made of Light, by the Light, in the Light, and for the Light. This book teaches methods to end the negative darkness and return your energy to the purity of the Light that is your birthright.

Negative interference, to give a basic definition, is the prevention of positive free will, which is every Be-ing's birthright and the birthright of the planet. To stop or prevent a harmful or violent act is not negative interference. To prevent someone's ability to do and live as one chooses, harming none, *is*. To force someone to do something they would not freely choose to do is negative interference, as well. A love spell, for example, pressures someone into a relationship she or he would not otherwise want. Psychic vampires drain other people's energy because they are too needy to create their own, while the people they violate become tired and ill. The negative mass consciousness of greed, violence, despair, and emotional pain becomes negative interference if the individual goes along with it, believes in it, and thinks and lives accordingly. A psychic attack—energy deliberately sent to block free action or do harm—is probably the prime example of negative interference, and is also evil. Negative interference can come out of evil, but can also come from ignorance. It often results from unchecked negative emotions like anger, rage, envy, or greed.

Negative interference causes harm. It blocks your self-determination and obstructs your ability to manifest your life purpose. If you have experienced repeated bad luck or ill health, negative interference from this life or some other can be the cause. What is sometimes jokingly called "bad karma" may in fact be negative interference, too. Constant depression or agitation, negative thinking or destructive thoughts, physical pain, chronic fatigue, dis-ease, emotional disturbance, and a life filled with fear, may all come from this source. Negative things done to us remain in our energy until they are removed or healed.

Evil is defined as the conscious lack of goodness and the absence of love. Wrong done with conscious intent to harm, to block free will or love, is evil. Without love there is no honoring of life or the free will of those who live. The absence of love, including self-love, is a prerequisite for evil, as a loving person does not do conscious harm or violate others' free will. The takeover of Earth creation for other planets' gain is evil. The mass killing of people for whatever reason is evil, and has happened repeatedly in Earth history. The prevalence of abuse on Earth is evil—abuse of children, women, elders, pets, and other animals, those of "other" races, religions, nations, and genders, and the abuse of the Earth herself. Evil is conscious harm committed to interfere with or prevent free will and love.

Love can be defined as life, and the honoring of the life force and the Light. It is goodness for goodness' sake. Love is respecting and supporting others' right to self-determination and freedom of thought and act. It is noninterference with others' choices and destinies, with others' bodies, emotions, minds, spirits, or lives. Love begins with self-love. If you cannot respect your own Be-ing, creation and life, you cannot respect and honor others'. Self-love is not narcissism but the beginning for clearing oneself of negative interference and ending the influence of evil in your life and Be-ing. Love means using your own Be-ing, your own life, choices, thoughts, and deeds as channels for the Light and life force.

One further definition and a clarification—suffering and evil are not the same. Evil is harm done by conscious intent for the purpose of preventing Light and love from manifesting on Earth or in a person. Suffering can be caused by evil or negative interference, but it mostly is not. Suffering in itself is not evil. While not pleasant to experience, it can have positive purpose, such to create compassion by showing one what pain means, or engender inner strength or teach ways of endurance. Suffering can be a method of learning or of fulfilling a life lesson agreed to for that time or lifetime. It can also be the means of presenting a situation for the purpose of resolving or ending it karmically.

Many people define suffering as karmic punishment, an eye for an eye sentencing in this life for past life misdeeds. They think that if you have raped or killed someone in a past life you will be raped or killed in turn in this one, or will suffer from deformity or dis-ease as a punishment. While this can sometimes be the case, it usually isn't. Karmic Law states that wrongs must be righted by learning not to repeat them again, by gaining the understanding of what you have done and why it is wrong. Sometimes this means a turn-around of suffering, with the person experiencing for herself what she has caused in others. More often, however, karmic suffering is the result of hurt, damage, or harm not healed from past lives and carried forward. The suffering will repeat until it is healed, and can be seen as an opportunity to find the healing and the resolution that ends it.

To repeat then, negative interference is violation of another's positive or harmless free will. It can come out of ignorance or negative emotion. If it comes out of direct intent to do harm, it is evil. Evil is the absence of love and is the conscious intent to do harm, or to prevent the manifesting of free will, Light, or love. Suffering may be caused by evil or the negative darkness but is not evil in itself. It can be karmic, or a way of learning compassion or a life lesson. There are various types of negative interference and evil, and the purpose of this book is teach the methods that prevent and end them.

Negative interference and evil can come from human and nonhuman sources, from Earth sources or sources beyond the Earth. While the origin of evil on this planet is the attempted hostile takeover of the Earth and Earth creation by other-planetary Be-ings, most negative interference is of human, this-planet origin. Some is deliberate and some is not. The negative mass consciousness of the planet, in major part created by that attempted takeover, is the source of negative interference by people against other people and against the Earth. The daily news is an example of that negative mass consciousness. We are steeped in stories of crime, violence, and disaster, so much so that we come to believe that the negativity is all there is. We begin to agree that the world is bad and act in accordance with that belief. We take part in it and are held down by it.

The negative mass consciousness includes defeatist and harmful beliefs and emotions, such as "There is not enough for everyone, so I have to take what I think is mine or someone else will take it from me." Or "Everyone is against me, other people are dangerous." Emotions of greed, envy, jealousy, anger, rage, revenge, ill will, despair, and hopelessness surround us. Sunk in these beliefs and emotions, we can only be effected in harmful ways. When someone directs them at us consciously, whether with the intent to harm or not, we are effected even more—they can be used to manipulate us. We can learn to protect ourselves from this energy and raise our own vibrations beyond the reach of this negative bombardment. We can also learn to reprogram our individual Mind Grids to change our own consciousness first and then the Mind Grid of the planet.

Some negative interference comes from people who did us harm in past lives. They reappear in this lifetime for our karma to be cleared and their negative effects ended and healed. Someone who has done harm to us in a past life, or several past lives, returns for the karma to be completed. Completing means stopping it, sometimes by simply refusing to allow the person to have further contact, by saying no. Sometimes what is needed is to understand what happened in the past, to recognize and understand a pattern and to ask for it to end. Sometimes the way to end the negative karma with an individual is to heal the damage that person has done to us, now and in ourselves. Techniques follow for doing these things. These evil or interfering Be-ings may be human or nonhuman, and sometimes objects from past lives can carry such karma. These objects are called artifacts.

One form of negative manipulation, violation of free will, is in negative spells, rituals, curses, symbols, or enchantments. While modern Women's and Goddess Spirituality and Wicca have ironclad ethics preventing this behavior, it was not always so in the past. Spells do not require a "witch" to cast them, and in fact those who do such things are not by definition Witches or Wiccans at all. Wicca is the positive religion of honoring the Goddess and the Light. Evil can be directed in these ways, and most of us have experienced it in past lives if not in this one. These attacks, and they are attacks, can be difficult to discover and remove, but they can be ended in our past, present, and future.

Psychic attacks are the sending of energy negatively for the purpose of harm. This can be done unconsciously, by very negative emotion directed at someone, or deliberately by conscious use of energy for specified or unspecified harm. The results can be minor if the person being attacked is sufficiently protected or the sender is weak or psychically untrained. The harm can be major if the recipient is unprotected or the sender is determined and psychically strong. Great harm and suffering can come this way and can continue through many lifetimes until the karma and damage are cleared. Pain traps that activate in specified situations can result. For example, something stops you every time you try to do your life's work. Returning these psychic attacks is not the way to deal with them. Becoming protected and clearing all karma with the sender is the ethically correct way to end them. Exchanging attack for attack in any sort of psychic war is dangerous and can only cause greater karma and more serious and lasting damage.

Human negative interference can come from someone who is no longer living, and this is called an entity or ghost. Ghosts usually mean no harm, but are simply lost souls who are unable to find where they should be. They may not know that they have died, and they may remain in a house they have lived in or near people they loved or hated. A ghost that enters the energy of a living person is a possession, and it can cause a great deal of damage and disruption. Some of these situations are evil but most are not. Most are simply spirits needing help. They may make a disturbance to get attention, so you will know they are there and give them what they need. They are usually easy to pass over to the Light for care and healing. The techniques to do this work follow later.

Some spirits are not and were never human. They can be displaced elementals—spirits of Earth, Air, Fire, Water, or Metal. They can appear as tornadoes and wildfires. While usually not evil, they are negative in the sense that they have great power and are in the wrong place. A bull in a china shop causes damage, and so do these. Whereas human spirits that are released and removed from the Earth and people's energy are passed over to the Light, these are passed under to the Fire at the Center of the Earth for purification and recycling. Other nonhuman entities, called attachments, are also passed under rather than over. They may be karmic suffering and karmic pain traps, random negative energy, the sources of some dis-eases, or simply misplaced nonhuman energies. They are not deliberate attacks.

Evil can also come from other planets. Everyone on Earth is carrying the result of damage and interference to the planetary creation and Mind Grid—we reflect the damage done to the Great Mother. Part of that evil is in its access to our energy, usually to reduce our Light, reduce our positive free will, create negative emotions and attitudes, and interfere with our life purposes and planetary service. Everyone suffers from this interference. It is now time for Earth to reclaim her purity, free will, and destiny in the Light. It is time to clear human energy of negative implants and mechanisms that work to control us and create fear in us. They reduce who we are and who we can become. Implants are devices carried in our energy over lifetimes that have the purpose of disrupting our lives and damaging our energy systems.

Alien evil involves multiple realities and dimensions, and between realities and dimensions. Please note that not all other-planetary energy and Be-ings are evil; most are our helpers and healers. We are multidimensional Be-ings who have lost most of our knowledge of who we are. Because we have lost so much, we are vulnerable and limited, and too easily preyed upon. This is about to end on Earth. Most negative interference, whether human, nonhuman or negative alien, occurs by crossing dimensions of existence. The Source of All Evil as it manifests on Earth is the renegade group of what are known as the Greys; they are the Be-ings that attacked Nada and Earth creation to take over this planet. They have failed to do so, but have caused untold damage, wars, harm, and suffering to all Earth Be-ings and Earth life for millenniums. They are from the Orion star system.

Their allies are the Orions themselves, sometimes known for their lizard form—their spaceships look like alligators and the Be-ings themselves. Orion implants and mechanisms project infestations of spiders, rats, snakes, jellyfish, squid, and other creepy-crawlies when seen in human energy. These are deceptive as they are only holograms from a central mechanism, usually a black box with trailing, curling wires, which is the real interfering object. Their purpose is to create fear, disruption, and damage to human energy systems, even at a very high core soul level. Orion implants reincarnate with us over countless lifetimes, until they are deactivated, removed, and destroyed.

Another source of evil on Earth is what I have named The Negative Form. This entity is one of the creations and manifestations of The Source of All Evil and has been the origin of most of the interfering evil working through negative people to do harm on Earth. Where deliberate psychic attacks are being sent, this is the driving force and source of sustaining damage. People allowing entrance of the Negative Form to their energy, or attacked by it, carry it over lifetimes until they become strong enough to reject it. The Negative Form causes continued suffering and continued harm, but is now being obliterated from this planet. Also now being obliterated are The Source of All Evil, Orion and all their creations and manifestations, as well as their interplanetary wars and interference for control of the Earth. There will be more discussion of all of these things later.

The symptoms of psychic interference, of negative interference in one's energy and life are a list and litany of most of human suffering. There is much to be cleared and protected from just about every human being. People who live in a state of chronic fear or oppression, anger, quarrelsomeness, conflict, agitation, and restlessness, confusion, despair, or feelings of doom, abandonment, wrong, or evil are likely to be carrying negative interference, implants, or psychic attacks. Chronic negative thinking is also a symptom of negative interference—hateful, destructive, or belittling thoughts, thoughts of suicide, voices with negative messages, voices with meanness or orders, sudden personality changes, and mental or nervous breakdowns. Memory loss, memory gaps, unusual seizures, and inability to concentrate are also symptoms of psychic attack, along with lack of motivation or interest in one's work and the inability to do one's work, lethargy, and the inability to make an effort or to exert one's will.

If everything seems to be going wrong in your life and life's work, if you are experiencing recurrent illnesses, chronic fatigue and exhaustion, unexplained body pains or marks, or suffering chronic poverty and restriction of abundance, negative interference is a possible reason. Wanting to sleep all the time or suffering serious insomnia, frequent or recurrent nightmares, and fear of sleeping are other symptoms of attack. The loss of psychic abilities and of normal contact with spirit guides, angels, your Goddess, or the Light is a definite indication of evil and negative interference. You may receive false psychic information and pendulums may not work accurately. You may feel negative closure, or constricted or burning feelings in your Crown Chakra or other chakras, or in any part of your body or energy. You may feel traumatized and afraid, without knowing why, and may also be in denial that anything is wrong.

You may experience enhanced psychic phenomena, but decidedly unpleasant ones. There may be psychic visions or dreams of bugs, alligators, or other creepy things on or around you, and of implants or black boxes with wires. There may be visions or dreams of monster Be-ings, or of people or animals with red, glowing eyes. You may see negative or attacking space-ships, evil flying things, mechanisms or pain traps, or negative objects in one's aura or chakras. You may have dreams or flash-backs of spaceship abductions. All these are of negative alien origin, from Orion or the negative Greys.

Ghosts or negative entities may cause poltergeist activity in your home—things breaking and falling, multiple or recurrent leaking water sources, outbreaks of fire, odors of decay or appearances of slime, odd footprints that seem to just disappear, odd unexplained sounds of no reasonable origin, or a sense of weight or oppression especially in or on your chest or heart. You may see the entities, or feel or hear them in your home, body, or energy. Pets' agitation, aggression, or bad behavior is often indication of a ghost-type entity, or of a psychic attack upon your home, as are plants or gardens blighted or dying.

Symptoms of spirit possession, of ghosts or discarnate entities inhabiting your body and energy, include fatigue and tiredness, moodiness, and personality changes, poor memory and concentration, sudden anxiety or depression, impulsiveness, unusual drug or alcohol abuse, negative or unknown inner voices, new and sudden physical problems, and negative reaction to discussions of possession.[1] Symptoms of alien abduction by the negative Greys are often preceded by UFO sightings, seeing an intense light, hearing crackling noises, floating out of body, paralysis, and night seizures. Abductions are followed by a period of lost time, an implanted memory that has nothing to do with abduction (called screen memory), body marks and scars, nosebleeds, dreams of the experience or their abductors, obsessive need to know what happened, insomnia and fear of sleeping,

---

[1] Edith Fiore, *The Unquiet Dead: A Psychologist Treats Spirit Possession* (New York: Ballantine Books, 1987), front page.

heightened psychic ability or psychic opening, and the discovery of implants and objects in the physical body.[2]

Reliance on the Light is the means of protection and clearing from all negative darkness, negative interference, and evil. The methods for doing so follow in this book. Negative interference is simply a fact of human existence, not to be feared but to be dealt with, not to hide from but to fight. The indications of protection from and clearing of negative interference are just as pronounced as the symptoms of attack and evil. They offer a difference, however, and the difference is joy and well-being. When you are cleared of evil and fully protected, you feel relaxed, calm, and at peace. You will experience restful sleep and increased vitality and wellness, a quiet mind, and a positive outlook, with a sense of safety and security. You will feel in control of your life and free will, and fully connected to your life's work and life path, your service to the planet.

Every aspect of your life and work will run smoothly, with fewer obstacles and fuller abundance. Your psychic abilities will be clear and open, accurately functioning, and you will experience connection with spirit guides, angels, the Goddess, the Lords of Karma and Ascended Masters, and with other Be-ings of the Light. You will be able to trust in your life, to trust in the future, and to trust in the Goddess and the Light. All these things are available to you, and they begin now. The time for negative interference, attack, and evil on the Earth is ending. By freeing yourself, you begin to free the planet, and goodness and Light will prevail.

---

[2] Marcus Day, *Aliens: Encounters with the Unexplained* (Chicago: Quadrillion Publishing Limited, 1997), pp. 79–82.

2

MEDITATION, VISUALIZATION, AND THE LORDS OF KARMA

Some basic skills are needed for the processes and methods of this book. Until now, psychic protection and clearing was involved and difficult, and often hit or miss. This is no longer the case. The methods presented in this chapter and used throughout this book are easy and highly effective. They go deeper than those used in the past, reaching both the effects and the sources of psychic interference and attack. They also involve clearing and protection from other-planetary negative darkness, as well as from that originating on this planet. Please remember, however, that while negative interference from Orion and the negative Greys have brought much suffering to Earth, it is also Be-ings from other planets that are protecting, defending, and healing us. Other-planetary positive assistance is now ending all disruption of Earth evolution.

This book is intended for intermediate to advanced level psychic workers and healers. Those who are beginning in metaphysics can also learn to use the processes and doing so will raise their development as psychics. It is important to do the processes exactly as given, without changing the wording. They can then be used for whatever requests you have, once the requests listed in each chapter are completed. I will begin with some basic information on meditation and visualization, since all psychic work depends on them, then continue with methods and processes that are more advanced and are totally new.

This book is a bridge between my *Essential Energy Balancing* (The Crossing Press, 2000) and the forthcoming *Healing the Goddess*. It is not necessary to have completed the work of *Essential Energy Balancing* to do the work that follows, but I recommend it. It is also helpful to have read and worked with the material in my book *We Are the Angels* (The Crossing Press, 1997). I always recommend Reiki to everyone in metaphysics and healing, as it is the basis for all healing methods. See my book *Essential Reiki* (The Crossing Press, 1995); it is best to have all three degrees or at least Reiki II. You may find my book *Psychic Healing with Spirit Guides and Angels* (The Crossing Press, 1996) helpful as well, though the methods that follow are quicker and easier. Psychic protection has been a focus in much of my previous work.

The primary difference from my previous books in the psychic protection methods that follow is that they are based on working with the Lords of Karma. These agents of the Goddess are the keepers of our soul records and requirements. They are Ascended Masters and members of the angelic realm. Ascended Masters are people who have completed all requirements to reincarnate on Earth and all other planets. They have learned all the karmic lessons that a multitude of lifetimes on Earth and other worlds can offer, and are now evolved enough to guide others—both individuals and planets. They are highly trained in their work. Each soul group has a group of the Lords of Karma to oversee their evolutionary growth. A Karmic Board coordinates all the Lords of Karma groups and makes final difficult decisions. The head of the Karmic Board and caretaker of all Earth Karma is Nada, our Great Mother and creator. The caretaker of karma beyond Earth incarnation, of incarnations in the Milky Way galaxy on planets beyond Earth's solar system, is Divine Director. The All Mother creator of the galaxy is Light Mother. She is the next higher authority after Divine Director and Nada, as well as the creator of the archangels. Divine Director's and Nada's creator and creator of the archangels, as well.

The Lords of Karma are of both sexes, all ages, all races, and all types of people. They appear as Earth Be-ings and all have had many incarnations on Earth. They are of the highest Light and the highest love. They are known to all of Earth's religions but are beyond all religious dogma. The Karmic Board consists of members of the Lords of Karma, as well as angels, archangels, and other Enlightened (Ascended) Be-ings. The many Goddesses are not part of the Lords of Karma or Karmic Board but work closely with them, and are often a bridge between the individual and the Karmic Board. The angels are our oversouls and individual protectors, and the archangels are planetary protectors and warriors against evil and the negative dark. These Be-ings have been assigned the task of overseeing Earth evolution, which also means the evolution of many individuals to create the critical mass necessary to raise the evolution of the planet.

Everyone who incarnates meets and works with the Lords of Karma before birth and in the between-life state. They are keepers of our Akashic Records, the records of each soul's many incarnations and development on Earth and all planets. We work with them closely to choose and design the learnings and situations of each lifetime, and to evaluate that lifetime's learning at its end. Our many incarnations are not random, but a careful course of study about being human and learning to love. They are also designed to teach us compassion, freedom, and independence, and planetary service and dedication. Nothing that happens in any lifetime is a mistake, it is all a part of the lessons. The point of most of these situations is in how we deal with them and whether or not we deal with them with love.

Karma is the process by which situations are repeated until the lesson is learned. There is no failure if the lesson is not learned in its initial lifetime, but karma that returns over several lifetimes becomes a pattern that is harder to clear. For example, someone who has been abused in one lifetime and does not learn personal empowerment by the end of that life will experience abuse again and (if necessary) again until she takes her own power. She is not supposed to become an abuser in an eye for an eye sense, but to refuse to be abused again and to heal the damage that abuse has caused in her body, emotions, mind, and spirit. Repeated damage over many lifetimes becomes core soul damage and many people are healing core soul damage from abuse at this time. Once a woman has healed the damage in herself she can help to heal it in others. When enough of the karma of abuse is cleared from enough people, abuse will be cleared from the planet, removed from the planetary Mind Grid.

This is the way karma works. It is not punishment but a mechanism for learning. The point of the learning is first to heal oneself, then to heal others and the Earth, and to remove suffering from everyone and from the planet. Until very recently, karma was something we were born with and had to live with. There was no escape and no release until the learning was completed and it was usually completed the hard way over a number of lifetimes. Today, however, things are different. We have been granted by Nada some very easy ways of requesting and achieving the release of karma that have never before been available or permitted. Because it is time for the Earth to evolve, and because Earth is in desperate need, we have been granted dispensation from the requirement to heal karma the long way. The methods for doing this are given in *We Are the Angels* and more thoroughly in *Essential Energy Balancing*, and they will be briefly repeated in this chapter.

With these new and simple methods, releasing karma is usually only a matter of properly making the request. When you do, the process of learning through living can be bypassed and the learning granted and completed almost instantly. What is necessary for this process is realization. By your realization that something is wrong in your life and you need healing of it, you acknowledge that you have learned the lesson and are ready to release the karma. If there is something more for you to know about the situation or its source, you will be given it. If there are things you must complete or be aware of first, you will be led to what you need to know or do. If you are refused a request, you may ask what is needed to have it accepted and will be told. Most refused requests, if they are for your best good, will be granted eventually.

Treat the Lords of Karma, and any other Masters, angels, archangels, Goddesses, or other Be-ings of the Light, with the utmost respect. I should not have to say this, but it bears saying. We are being given gifts of a magnitude that you have no idea of as yet. Always say thank you. Always say please. Never argue. Most negative responses can be reversed, if you ask for guidance as to what is needed or wait for further understanding or healing. We are being granted Enlightenment by these processes, release from being required to reincarnate, and release from all suffering. We are being granted protection and healing from some very real and very destructive evil. And we are being given back our self-determination and free will, and control of our own planet. Thank the Lords of Karma and all those who come to help you.

Divine Director is the keeper and guardian of karma in this galaxy that is not of our solar system. (Divine Director is his title, rather than his name.) We have had many series of incarnations on more planets than Earth. The human soul is ancient beyond imagining and has lived and died thousands of times. Once our current Earth karma is fulfilled or released and healed, we must address the healing of karma remaining from other-planet lifetimes. These involve anything that is left after working with the Lords of Karma over a period of time. If the Lords of Karma agree to release something, but the situation still remains months later on, it's a pretty safe bet that the source is from an other-planet incarnation. Divine Director is the one to address for its release and for healing of the source lifetime.

The easiest way to do this is simply to ask for both the Lords of Karma and Divine Director with each request for karmic release. If something is Earth karma only, and you need to know that, you will be told. If something is other-planet karma you may or may not be told but the situation will be healed if your request is granted. You will usually not be shown the other-planet situation. Working with Divine Director and other-planet karma is new to this book, and a new process for Earth as well. With Divine Director's help, all of a soul's karma can be cleared and healed, and full protection from all sources of evil and negative interference can be given.

The key to karmic release is in our DNA. The DNA is the transmitter of karma over all of a soul's incarnations and lifetimes on all planets. It is programmed from the individual Mind Grid as well as from the Mind Grid of the Earth. It does much more than carry forward physical genetic traits such as eye color and inherited dis-eases. The DNA replicates karmic programming, and some or most negative interference is transmitted over lifetimes by replication through the DNA. The DNA also regulates the amount of Light a human energy system can rise to and hold, thereby regulating individual and planetary evolution. When enough people raise their Light vibration, a critical mass is reached to raise it for the planet. The key to doing this is also through the DNA.

On Earth we are said to have two strands of DNA, a double helix. Before the Greys' attack on this planet's creation, however, we were destined to have twelve strands of DNA for use in our Earth incarnations. The reconnection and healing of these twelve strands is required for the healing of Earth karma and completion of our incarnations on Earth. Earth Ascension, therefore, requires twelve strands of healed, reconnected, and fully reactivated DNA. Once twelve strands of DNA are activated, we also activate our other-planet karma for incarnations through our galaxy, the Milky Way. It requires twenty-one strands of fully healed, reconnected, and reactivated DNA to clear our other-planet karma. Yet, we still have more to go.

When twenty-four strands of DNA are healed, reconnected, and fully activated, we are no longer subject to negative interference on Earth of any kind, from any this-planet or other-planet source. It requires thirty-eight strands of DNA (healed, reconnected, and fully activated) to heal our creational damage as replicated from the damage to planetary creation, the planetary Mind Grid, and to Nada herself by the Source of All Evil. Yet the full complement of our DNA is even more than thirty-eight strands. It can be as high as 81 strands, but not for everyone, and the number of strands to reconnect will differ among individuals. The way to reconnect the proper amount of DNA for each individual is to simply make a request to the Lords of Karma and Divine Director to "clear, heal, reconnect, and fully activate the full complement of your DNA." You will be taken through this process in this chapter.

Once the request is made the process begins. It will take a period of time, about six months to complete. The request need only be made once. This reconnection is the means of clearing your Earth and other-planet karma, as well as clearing and protecting you from negative interference and evil of all types and from all sources. It is the central request for using this book and is crucial to all that follows. The reconnection is necessary for the release of all but the simplest of Earth karmas. With this reconnection, your ability to hold Light and raise your Light vibration increases exponentially. With this reconnection in a critical mass of individuals, the planet's vibration is raised and ascended—freed of the requirement to reincarnate—as well, thereby freeing all Earth Be-ings.

For those who have not previously learned it, meditation is the state needed for all psychic work, protection, and clearing work, and for working with the Lords of Karma and Divine Director, too. Most people are aware of meditation in some form, and only a very brief explanation will be given here. There are many methods of meditation and many books available on the subject, but for the purposes of this book the method is simply a calming and going within so that you can receive psychic information and instruction.

To begin with, meditation requires a quiet and protected space in a silent room. This is a place where you will not be disturbed and where you will learn to contact and work with the Lords of Karma, Divine Director, and other Be-ings of the Light. You may create an altar to your Goddess or to the Earth as a focus point, and may wish to cast a Circle of Protection for the room when you work. In chapters that follow, these processes will be explained. You may wish only to light a candle, which is a symbol of the Light and a good meditative focus and calming device. You may choose to do none of these things, but simply to become calm and still inside without using these tools. Until you have completed the house protection of Chapter 4, it is a good idea to simply request protection from the Light when beginning to meditate. State that only energies of the highest Light be allowed to participate in your work.

The last thing at night before bedtime is a good time to work, as psychic energy is stronger at night and you will be more relaxed and receptive. Close the door to your meditation room, unplug the telephone and TV, and insist that others in the house not enter or disturb you while you work. Pets may remain, as they are protectors and can help to hold the energy for you. If they decide to go, let them. Take a comfortable seated position on the floor or in a straight chair. Place your feet firmly on the floor when seated in a chair, or your buttocks firmly on the ground. Do not cross your arms or legs. Relax your body as much as possible. Light your candle and relax your mind. Agree to release all worries and earth-plane concerns and to clear your mind fully of all thoughts. Become still inside, still your mind, take a few deep breaths.

Now ask for grounding. To do this, imagine a grounding cord or line running from your genitals to the center of the Earth, to the Well of Life and Fire of Life at the planetary core. Rock your body once or twice from side to side, then forward and back. You will experience a calm centeredness that may be new to you, and that will enable you to quiet your mind and your body. These things are simple once you get the hang of them and are important. Imagining the grounding cord is the beginning of a skill related to meditation and also important for this work, that of visualization. This is the ability to gain psychic sensory information. It will seem as if you have "imagined" it, but imagination is visualization, and both are real.

It is important here to tell you that what you visualize, especially in the meditative state, you create and draw to you. Therefore, only imagine, visualize, or create positive things. The worst scenario you create in your mind you also create in your life. While not everything you see in meditation, in working with the Lords of Karma, or in psychic protection work is positive, you will not create negative scenes to complicate the issue. By visualizing the positive and not creating the negative, the negative scenes you do see will be shown only as information of what you need to clear or heal. Understand them as pain leaving, and use your visualization ability to promote their leaving forever. When negative scenes appear, you will call upon the Light.

Now, in the meditative state, ask to speak with the Lords of Karma and Divine Director. You will be given some psychic sensory perception of their presence. Visualization includes all sensory perceptions. Some people receive psychic information by seeing it, while others hear it, feel it, or just know that it is there. Some people receive physical sensations in their bodies of the Lords of Karma, perhaps feelings of warmth or tingling. Some perceive waves of color or Light, hear music, or simply feel at peace. Clear hearing is probably the most desirable way of perceiving, as it offers the most easily understood information. Whatever way you perceive, however, will give you what you need.

Ask the Lords of Karma and Divine Director to show you what a yes response will look or feel like when you work with them. When you understand what you are given, ask what a no response will look or feel like. Sometimes a no is no response at all. It is important to understand the yes and no before going further and this should be easy. If you have difficulty after several attempts, try using a pendulum to obtain your yes and no responses, making sure that it is the Lords of Karma and Divine Director who are running it. Remember to stay relaxed and to keep your mind clear of other thoughts and concerns.

A pendulum is any small weight on a short string or light chain. A necklace pendant works fine, as does a button or a metal washer on a string, but most metaphysical people prefer a brass weight or crystal on the bottom end and a bead on the top end of the chain. Hold the small end or free end of the string or chain, allowing the weight to swing free. Pendulums need to be kept very energetically clear to be accurate. Do this by submerging them in dry salt at least overnight before using. Most people who use pendulums have several, changing off frequently, and keeping them in salt to clear while not in use. Dedicate your pendulum to the Light (simply by saying so) and ask the Lords of Karma and Divine Director if they will run the pendulum for you. Ask the pendulum for a yes response; it will swing in a distinctive way. Ask for a no response; it will swing in a different way. These responses can be used to obtain psychic information or work with the Lords of Karma. Ask if they are there before starting, and go ahead with your requests only with a yes.

When you understand a yes and no response, whether in meditation or with the pendulum, you are ready to begin working with the Lords of Karma and Divine Director and the processes of psychic protection for this book. Remember to thank them for working with you and for each granted (or refused) request. Develop a cooperative relationship with your Lords of Karma group. Ask to speak with the Lords of Karma and Divine Director (use these precise words). When you perceive their presence, make the following request:

I ask the Lords of Karma and Divine Director to clear, heal, reconnect, and fully activate the full complement of my DNA.

When the response is yes, state:

I ask for these healings through the Mind Grid level, the DNA level, the Karmic Contract level, the Core Soul level and beyond, and through the Ascension level.

You will get a response for each of this list. If you receive a no, stop and clear it. To do so, first ask if the request or the step is needed. If it isn't, skip that level. If it is, or for a no to your original request, ask what you need to do to receive the yes. You will be told what to do or the information will come into your awareness. If there is something to be released first, use this process to release it, then make your request again. For example, if you are told that you cannot reconnect the full complement of your DNA, ask what you need to do. You may be told that there is a past life to clear, or shown a situation. Whether you understand what you are shown or not, ask for healing and release from it. Go through the full process with that request, then go through it again asking for the reconnection of the DNA. Use this any time you receive a no response, unless they tell you that your request or a level of it is not needed. Sometimes when you receive a no, waiting a moment, then asking again, will change the response to yes.

When you have a yes to all of the above, state:

I ask for this healing from beyond the Moment of Self to below the Center of the Earth, and from beyond the Pure Light above Creation to below the Well of Life and the Fire of Life at the Center of the Earth and all planets, and beyond and between all of these.

When you have a yes, state:

I ask to seal this healing unto the Light and unto Protection forever.

The Moment of Self is the point from which the soul individuates from the Light, the Goddess, and becomes its own awareness and own Be-ing. We ask to extend the healing to the Center of the Earth, as during our time of Earth incarnation we are a part of the planet and also working in service to it. The Pure Light above Creation is as far out there as I can envision our soul connections. The Well of Life and Fire of Life at the Earth's core are the receptacles for our life force and all of life on the planet. All planets have a Well of Life and a Fire of Life at their core. To seal the healing means to have it forever. You will only ask to seal things you wish to keep and will not use this part of the request when clearing your energy. If you are given a no to sealing unto the Light, just skip it. Accept the no; there is no need to release it.

When you have a yes to everything so far, finish the request as follows by stating:

I ask for these healings: Through all the levels and all the bodies, All the lifetimes on Earth and on all other planets, Including the present lifetime, Heal all the damage, And bring the healing into the present NOW.

If you receive a yes to this last section, the process is finished for Earth and most other-planet karma. If you receive a no, ask line by line to find the no and release it as above. It may take a complete new request to do so. Once the no is released, finish the process and it will usually be granted. For all steps of the request above use the exact wording as given. Use this process for all Lords of Karma requests in this book. Be sure to say thank you at the end of each request.

No more is needed for the clearing of karma. This sounds amazing, but it is so. Besides the protection processes, the method can be used—and should be used—to heal everything that needs healing in your life. Everyone has situations they wish they didn't have to live with. This is your opportunity to release them. Use this process to request release and healing for four primary categories of karma: to heal your relationships with all the people in your life (alive or not), to heal life situations (your poverty or lack of life purpose, for example), character traits (like being a smoker or drinker, or a poor listener), and dis-eases (do these last, after looking at everything else that needs work).

I cannot begin to tell you how important it is to work with the Lords of Karma to heal everything that is wrong in your life. This is the most important thing you can do and the most profound healing you will ever receive. If you only request the full complement of your DNA you will heal your life profoundly. If you only do the processes in this book, you will protect yourself profoundly. But if you do it all, you will heal yourself totally. Never be afraid to ask for something that you wish for, but be very careful in your asking. What you ask for you will get.

In the case of relationships, ask for karmic healing for every conflicted relationship you have or have ever had. Use the request, "I ask for karmic healing for my relationship with (name)." For a few relationships you will ask for karmic severance, which means to end your Earth relationship with that person forever. Save this for your incest perpetrator, stalker, or other negative people. If you ask to "cancel all karma and all karmic contracts from Earth and all planets with (name)," you will end all contact, harm, and karma with that person forever on Earth and all planets. Ask permission of the Lords of Karma and Divine Director before requesting either of these, and only proceed with their permission. If granted, the request is irrevocable.

Also ask to heal the karma of your relationship with those people who are close and near to you. Doing so clears all other-life karma and conflicts and makes the relationship even closer and more harmonious. You will spend a great deal of time discussing relationships with the Lords of Karma and Divine Director. Relationships are our primary way to learn how to love, and learning to love is a primary purpose of incarnation on Earth. Clear and heal the karma of all the relationships you can, with everyone who comes to mind. You will remember friends and enemies you have not thought about since childhood. You will understand what these relationships have given you and how they have changed or hurt you. You will uncover some very negative relationships that you will clear later. Just ask for karmic release, karmic severance, or to cancel all karma and karmic contracts with them now.

There is no other way to clear karma immediately than in the above process. The granting of this process to us is a great gift to every individual who makes use of it and to the evolution of people and the Earth. The protection processes of this book can usually be done in other ways, but doing them through the Lords of Karma and Divine Director is the easiest way, and the most effective. Why not take the easiest and quickest way?

Once a request is granted, it can take up to three weeks for total clearing, though some responses are immediate. If you ask to cancel all karma and karmic contracts with a person or situation, and the karma is not from Earth, you will find your Crown Chakra closed up for four hours for the repatterning of your DNA and Mind Grid. It feels strange but there is nothing to fear. Do most of your karmic release work at bedtime so any closing up will be over by morning. It will not interfere with your earthplane work but will hamper your psychic abilities temporarily.

These releases are a tremendous gift that will change your life in every positive way. Think carefully about what to ask for and remember that what you ask for you will get. The Lords of Karma will not allow you to be harmed by any mistake you make, but the experience may teach you a bit of a lesson. If you realize you have asked wrongly, ask them if it's best to revoke it and if you may. This work is individual work; you may not do it for someone else. If on occasion you wish to ask for help for someone else, go to Divine Director. He will grant your request only if it is for the best good and according to the free will of the person receiving it. Never violate another's free will, not even for what you think is their good. To violate this Karmic Law is to bring negative karma upon yourself. While you are learning to clear yourself of negative interference be careful never to interfere with other people's freedom of will.

With these basic processes completed, the next chapter begins your psychic protection.

3

YOU ARE GODDESS

"You are Goddess" is a Wiccan saying that is certainly true. We are all created by Goddess and in our highest Energy Selves we are all Her incarnations. The Goddess has many names from many cultures and countries but all the Goddesses are One. In our stepped-down, incarnated physical form, we forget who we are and have too little contact with the higher levels of our Be-ing. *Essential Energy Balancing* was created to reconnect you with who you really are. In *Reliance on the Light*, with its focus on psychic protection, reconnection to Goddess and Her Light is the very first step. This reconnection is done by dedication.

When you dedicate yourself to the Goddess and the Light you are making this statement to the Universe: "I am a Be-ing of Light and anything not of the Light must leave." You are stating that you have chosen to awaken your higher Be-ing, to reclaim who you are. You are putting the negative dark on notice that it is no longer welcome and will no longer be tolerated in your energy or your life. This is a serious statement to make. It will draw the Light to fill and protect you, but it may also draw the negative dark to challenge you. The negative dark will not want to give up any hold it may have upon your energy. It may try to block your Light; it may try to claim a stronger hold. The state-ment seems to begin a battle of good and evil for your freedom, but the battle has been going on for many millenniums and the Light has already won.

Dedicating yourself to the Goddess may start a period of chaos in your life. You may change your job, your mate, your friends, the town you live in, and some basic ways that you think—all very suddenly. Your psychic abilities will develop in ways that can be disconcerting. You may feel that you have lost the stability you once had. However, all this stirring up is simply rearranging. The things that have held you back, the negative dark, is leaving, making way for new ideas and positive growth. The process is similar to what happens to people in the year after receiving a Reiki II attunement, or after completing Essential Energy Balancing I. By making the dedication, or receiving the attunement, or completing the Energy Balancing, you have opened yourself up to healing and change. There is another Wiccan saying about the Goddess: "She changes everything She touches, and everything She touches changes." Yet I have never met anyone who chose to revoke her dedication, or to go back to a former self.

Dedicating yourself to the Goddess is the first step in the daily ongoing protection of your energy and home. The Goddess is pure unconditional love and pure compassion, and opening yourself to Her brings these qualities into you. Doing so promotes a positive attitude of compassion, and love that is the most important thing you can do to place yourself above human and nonhuman negativity, negative interference, and evil. An attitude of compassionate love keeps others' emotions of anger, resentment, jealousy, judgment, hate, victim-thinking, fear, negative desire, and envy away from you. It prevents these emotions from affecting your energy and your life. Having compassion for yourself and all others, a sense of positive worth, and a rejection of guilt, blame, and judgment all raise your energy

41

vibration toward the Goddess Light and away from those who can use negative emotions to harm you. Dedicating yourself to the Goddess is the initiation of this process.

By choosing an attitude of well-being, generosity, security, cooperation with others, and acceptance of who you are, you place yourself fully in the Light. You remove yourself from others' negativity while ending your own. Dedication is the statement that affirms this choice. It is best to further the process of raising your energy beyond negative emotions by asking to clear them from your karma. Go to the Lords of Karma and Divine Director and ask for the following things, one at a time. Ask for karmic release from all negative and defeatist emotions. Ask for karmic release from judgment of oneself and all others; from negative guilt and blame (of yourself and others); from anger, resentment, rage, jealousy, envy, hate, victim-thinking, fear, and negative desire. Each one of these requests is a new Lords of Karma process.

Ask the Lords of Karma and Divine Director to release you from the punishment and reward belief system that is so prevalent in Western thought. By expecting to be punished, you punish yourself, and draw punishment to you from the outside. Remember that the Light does not punish at all, it only teaches you the lessons you came here to learn. Karma is not punishment but teaching. By expecting reward, you wait for recompense that may or may not come. The recompense is only in the living and doing. You look at others and wonder uselessly why they have the benefits they have received, and why they are or are not punished. To release yourself from this punishment and reward belief system is healing and freeing, and it releases you from judgment of yourself and others.

Next ask to bring the following positive qualities, qualities of the Goddess and the Light, fully into your life. Word the

42

requests this way: "I ask to be healed of all that prevents me from my fullest expression of (fill in some of the following)." Some of the qualities to ask for, one by one, are: unconditional love, compassion for oneself and all others, a healed and open heart, a positive outlook, positive self-worth and self-image, wellness and well-being, generosity towards oneself and all others, a sense of security and peace in your life, cooperation with others, and acceptance of who you really are. You will think of other negatives to release and positive qualities to add, and are encouraged to request them. It may take several nights of meditation to complete these requests, which are preliminaries to your dedication.

Making these karmic requests, and then doing the dedication that follows, brings the Radiance of the Light Beyond the Goddess into your energy. It allows that Light to fill you and to heal your aura, removing negativity and reinforcing all good qualities. The first defense against negativity and negative interference is an aura filled with Light. This radiating Light will heal a great deal of the damage to your aura caused by negative emotions, yours and others', and will begin to protect you from the entrance of further negativity. Ask the Lords of Karma and Divine Director to fill your aura with so much Light that no negativity or evil can enter, exist, or remain in your energy or Be-ing. This is a good request to repeat often.

The aura is the envelope of Light that surrounds your physical body. It is composed of energy, layered like the skin of an onion. Each ascending layer vibrates faster than the one below it, and each ascending layer holds more Light. When you request more Light, you raise your energy vibration and the vibration rate of each auric layer. The more Light your aura holds, the less negative energy can affect it or stick to it. The higher your overall vibration, the higher your Light, the less the

43

negative dark can harm you. Some aura damage is karmic or creational and the above processes begin the healing. Light filling the aura protects it. Each process that follows in this book serves to heal a damaged aura, to reinforce, defend, and protect it from negativity, negative interference, and evil.

When you first begin to raise your vibrational rate, first dedicate yourself to the Light, and request the end of negative thinking and the increase in positive qualities, it will seem that more negative happenings occur in your life for a while. This is because you have stirred the sludge at the bottom of the pot. You are shaking things up to create change. For a while the soup seems muddy, but only for a while. When things settle, the overall quality of the water in the pot is far clearer than it was before. Each step in karmic healing and bringing in the Light stirs the pot a little further, until there is no more sludge left. If negative thoughts, visions, or happenings occur, view them as pain leaving and watch them pass.

You may find at this time that someone in your life becomes very angry with you, seemingly without cause. Raising the vibration of your aura and filling it with Light prevents others from draining you. These people are called "psychic vampires." They are usually needy people who are unaware that they are causing harm. They may draw from your energy because they think they don't have enough of their own, because they are too lazy to create their own, or because they think you or the world owes them a free ride. Raising your vibration shakes these people out of your energy, and someone who has been using you in this way will often be angry when their game is up. You may be aware of who these people are. When you spend time with them you notice *them* brightening, but when you leave them *you* feel unusually tired or depressed. Stand firm and do not allow them to reattach themselves to you. If they attempt to, fill yourself with more Light. They will be just fine on their own.

When you have completed the list of karmic requests above, and before or after your dedication to the Goddess and the Light, you may wish to protect yourself from the planetary mass consciousness that is so negative at this time. The planet and planetary Mind Grid are weighed down with scenarios of disaster, hopelessness, and doom. Television, the media, and the movies are the worst offenders for creating and perpetrating this. Remember that what you think and visualize, you create and draw to you. By making the above requests to heal yourself of negativity and reinforce the positive in your life, you have begun to heal your own Mind Grid. When enough people do this and a critical mass is reached, the planetary Mind Grid is affected and changed for the better. The planetary Mind Grid is the consensus of the thinking of most of the people who live on Earth. In the meantime, it is best to protect your energy from the negativity.

The reconnection of your full DNA is the best and ultimate way to protect you from the negativity of the planet. This will take some time, however. It is good to acknowledge to the Lords of Karma and Divine Director that you recognize that the planetary consensus is negative and want to rise above it. The higher the vibration of your aura and the more Light filling it, the further above this negativity you can go. Escaping the planetary mass consciousness is difficult and a little help is a good idea. Making the request to the Lords of Karma also tells them that you recognize your part in the problem and are ready to heal it in yourself. By doing this, you make the first step in healing it for the Earth and everyone on it. This is no small thing.

Therefore, ask to speak to the Lords of Karma and Divine Director and make the following request. Ask them to "raise your Light and energy vibration forever beyond the point where the negativity of the planetary mass consciousness can reach or affect you." Using the full Lords of Karma process for the above, also ask that you be fully healed of all damage resulting from the negative mass consciousness to all the levels and systems of your Be-ing. Ask to clear and purify your energy of all planetary mass consciousness negativity through all levels and all systems of your Be-ing now and forever, past, present, and future. Use the wording I have given for these requests. Each is a separate Lords of Karma and Divine Director process. You will feel great changes in your energy, great relief, and as your aura clears and fills with Light you will experience a greater well-being and inner peace than you ever have before. These are essential protection processes.

You are now ready to dedicate yourself to the Goddess and the Light. You may make the dedication to a particular Goddess, to the Great Goddess, or simply to The Goddess. If you do not wish to accept Goddess energy, you may dedicate yourself only to the Light. I am presenting the process below as a ritual in the Wiccan tradition, but you may do it differently if you wish. This is a sacred moment and dedication is as sacred an action as you can take. A ritual carries great power in that it acknowledges and enhances the sacredness of this life-changing and life-affirming act. You will create a sacred space, a space protected from the negative dark, but open and inviting to the positive darkness and the Light. Both are present in any ritual. Ritual can be defined as action taken into the body. It is the original meaning of magick, the changing of consciousness by will. Remember also that the first and ultimate sacred space is your body and your self, your own Be-ing.

Do this ritual at night before bed. It is done in your meditation room and in the meditative state. See that you are alone and undisturbed while accomplishing it. The best time to do a dedication ritual is on the night of the Full Moon; check a calendar for the next Full Moon date. The New Moon is also a positive time, but New Moon power is more erratic and less joyful than the Full. The night before Candlemas, Candlemas Eve, February 1, in Wicca is the traditional time for dedication, but if you are reading this in June and may not wish to wait till February, go ahead. A dedication to the Light is positive whenever you may do it. I made my first dedication on Candlemas Eve, 1978, and I renew it each year. The first time began a process of total change in my life that still continues, and every renewal feels better and better.

To prepare, the first step is to create an altar. This is a representation of Earth, Air, Fire, Water, and Spirit, a microcosm of the Universe to bring into your meditation space and into your life. An altar requires thought, as does every aspect of ritual and dedication, but it can be extremely simple. Choose an item that is meaningful to you to represent each of the five elements and the four directions. For Earth you may consider a potted plant, a crystal, a rose in a vase, a handful of soil on a dish, a small globe of the planet, or any representation of the pentacle—the Wiccan five-pointed star with its central point facing upward. Anything that comes from the Earth or the soil is a representation of the Earth element and also representative of the North. For the element of Fire, the South, try a lighted candle in a secure candle holder. Wait until you begin your ritual to light it.

For Air, the East, the traditional choice is to burn a stick or cone of incense in a small burner, or on a dish filled with sand or uncooked rice for heat insulation. Sage and cedar are traditional in Native American rituals for protection and the dispelling of negative energies. Sweetgrass invites in helpful spirits. Nag champa, an incense from India, is popular, too. Use natural herbs rather than synthetic or fruity fragrances. These herbs are inexpensive and available at herb shops, Native American stores, and metaphysical outlets. If your smoke detector is in your meditation room and you burn incense, take the detector to another room before beginning. There is nothing less conducive to sacred space than the sound of the alarm going off. If you are allergic to incense you may choose a beautiful feather to represent Air. Your symbol for water, the West, can be a bowl or glass of water with a bit of salt in it, a cup of wine, a bottle of essential oil, a seashell, or any object from the ocean or the beach.

The direction of Center, the center of the Circle, represents Spirit, life, or the soul. Use your imagination. Another candle is a possibility, a photograph or image of a Goddess, a single rose, a crystal sphere or empty bowl, some representation of a spiral, or a small unicorn statue. This element represents the Void, the place of emptiness and darkness from which all life descends. It is the planet's womb, the positive darkness, the source of life and Light. It is magick.

Besides the items for the Four Directions and the Center, you can add any other things to the altar that you wish. Among the objects, your altar should include a candle and matches, incense with burner, and a small glass or bowl of salt water. You may wish to include an essential oil for the Self-Blessing. You will use these things in the course of doing your ritual. I like to add a vase with a single live flower or bouquet in it to any ritual altar.

Choose and assemble the items, and arrange them on a cloth-covered table, dresser, or on the floor. They should be placed so that you can see them at eye level while doing your work. You should be able to reach them easily. Learn where north, south, east, and west are in your meditation room, and arrange the objects of your altar so that the item representing Earth is in the North, the one for Fire is below it in the South, the object for

Water is in the Western direction, and the item representing Air is in the East. The object representing Spirit is placed in the center of the circle made by the other four elements. Arrange these things in a pleasing and attractive manner.

Now prepare yourself. Begin by taking a cleansing bath that contains a cup of sea salt in the water. The bath is part of the ritual and is a step toward purifying your energy. Allow it to take some time, at least fifteen or twenty minutes, and enter and remain in the meditative state while taking it. Rinse the salt off, dry yourself and come to your ritual without clothing, or wearing only a loose robe if the room is too cold. You may wear a piece of Goddess jewelry or a pentacle, if you wish. Let your hair hang free and unconfined. Coming before the Light naked is a statement of trust, and a presenting of yourself as you really are. All human bodies are beautiful, no matter what size, shape, type, condition, age, or color. We are all one before the Goddess and that oneness is great beauty. Your body is sacred space and is the altar of your soul.

Stand or sit before your altar and get grounded and centered. Enter the meditative state, if you have not already done so, and light your candle. Light your incense and fan some smoke over your body as a ritual purification. Then fan the smoke over your altar and ritual objects. Take each of the objects representing the elements and one by one, hold them up to the candle flame. Pass them above the flame, and say, "I dedicate this object to the Light and to the Goddess." You may name each object and its element and direction as you do so. Note that the words of your ritual may be spoken aloud or silently. Next, ask for the presence and protection of the Guardians of the Four Directions, plus the Center, Above and Below. Ask them to create for you a Circle of Protection, a safe and sacred space. Visualize a circle of Light forming around you. This is the act of Casting the Circle, and you may not leave that circle now until your ritual is complete and the Guardians are released. Within that magick circle no negativity may enter.

Only those you invite may enter a Circle of Protection. Invite The Lords of Karma, Divine Director, your spirit guides, Guardian Angels of the Light, your Goddess, and anyone else you wish to be there. Declare the circle open to the Light, and only to those Be-ings of the highest Light. You may invite a totem animal, a living pet, ancestors, or friends, but it is best that you do the ritual without other living people present this first time, or at least without other people in body in the room. You are inviting Be-ings of the Light and spirit to witness your dedication, your commitment to the Light and to the Goddess, your commitment to become all that you can be.

Now make the statement that is the reason for your ritual: "I dedicate myself to the Light and to the Goddess forever. I dedicate myself to love." No more is needed, but you may add more if you wish. Remember that this dedication is a sacred vow. Do not make it lightly or make it at all if you fear it or do not truly choose it. You are making a vow in front of sacred witnesses, in front of the Lords of Karma. What you do has consequence. It also has great joy.

Follow your dedication with the Wiccan Self-Blessing, a simple and beautifully powerful statement of its own. Take a drop of salt water or incense ash on your index finger. You may also use an essential oil, olive oil, wine, or menstrual blood. These should be on the altar before you begin your ritual. Do the following steps:

WICCAN SELF-BLESSING

• Touch the fluid to your Crown Chakra (at the top of your head) and say:

Bless me Mother for I am your child and I am a part of you.

• Touch the fluid to your Third Eye (your forehead above and between your eyes) and say:

Bless me Mother that I may see you and may see my way.

• Touch the fluid to your lips or Throat Chakra and say:

Bless me Mother that I may speak your truth.

• Touch the fluid to your Heart Chakra and say:

Bless me Mother that my heart be whole and open.

• Touch the fluid to your Solar Plexus (your upper abdomen) and say:

Bless me Mother that my will be pure.

• Touch the fluid to your Belly Chakra (below the navel) and say:

Bless me Mother that my womb be filled with joy.

• Touch the fluid to your Root Chakra (at your vagina or genitals) and say:

Bless me Mother that I be grounded in the Earth.

• Touch the fluid to the bottoms of both feet and say:

Bless me Mother that I may walk in your path and fulfill my own.

•Touch the fluid to the palms of both hands and say:

Bless me Mother that I may do your work which is my own.

• Touch the fluid once more to your Crown Chakra and say:

Bless me Mother for I am your child and I am a part of you.

You may end the ritual here and open your Circle, or may continue with the following requests to the Lords of Karma and Divine Director. If you end the ritual now, do these exercises during your next nightly meditation session. Ask the Lords of Karma and Divine Director to grant you a Guardian Angel to protect you from negativity and harm. Ask to meet your Guardian Angel. Sit in meditation talking with your angel for a while. Ask your angel's name, and if your angel has a message or a task for you. You will call upon this angel whenever you need protection or clearing, so get to know who is there. Ask how you can best contact and work with your angel in the future. Remain in the meditative state to receive this information.

Now ask the Lords of Karma and Divine Director if you may meet and speak with your Goddess. You may already know who She is, but if not, ask Her now. Again sit in meditation, speaking with your Goddess. Ask Her for a message and ask Her how you can be in deeper and more frequent contact with Her. Now that you have dedicated yourself to Her, She will be much more present in your consciousness and in your life. Begin a relationship with your Goddess. She will not accept worship from you, but expects a cooperative and co-creative relationship. She is a friend and a sister; She is the highest part of who you are, your highest Be-ing. Get to know Her. You will learn to know Her more as time goes on and to make Her a part of every aspect of your daily reality. Approach your Goddess with the greatest respect and love, as She is love Herself.

It is best to end your ritual here. This is a lot for one session, especially if it is your first experience with Casting a Circle. To complete your ritual, thank your Goddess, Guardian Angel, the Lords of Karma, and Divine Director for being there and for the gifts they have given you. Thank the Guardians of each of the Four Directions, plus the Center, Above and Below, releasing them from the circle. Thank all the Be-ings of Light who have been in the circle with you. The traditional Wiccan blessing to end a ritual is: "The Circle is open but unbroken. Merry meet and merry part, and merry meet again. Blessed Be." It means this ritual is over, but not ended. We have come together in joy and we now part in joy, and we will meet in sacred space once more. "Blessed Be" is a benediction, both asking for and offering peace, goodness, and love.

You may Cast a Circle nightly to do your meditation and your work with the Lords of Karma and Divine Director if you wish. It is not necessary or recommended, however. Casting a Circle is a special event, done for special occasions. The traditional times in Wicca for doing formal ritual are at the New and Full Moons and the eight Sabbats or holidays of the cycle of the year. Rituals for the Sabbats are usually done the evening before the holiday, except the ritual for the Wiccan New Year of Hallows Eve which is done on October 31. The eight Sabbat dates are Hallows Eve (October 31), Winter Solstice (December 19–22, see a calendar for each year's date), Candlemas (February 2), Spring Equinox (March 19–22), Beltane (May 1), Summer Solstice (June 19–22), Lammas (August 1), and Fall Equinox (September 19–22).

For much more information on the Wheel of the Year, see my book *Casting the Circle: A Women's Book of Ritual* (The Crossing Press, 1990), or Starhawk's *The Spiral Dance: A Rebirth of the Ancient Religion of the Great Mother* (Harper and Row, 1979). Many other good books on Wicca and Women's Spirituality are available. If you prefer not to invoke the Goddess in your protection and in your life, simply do your dedication to the Light.

While Casting a Circle is a formal way to invoke protection and the Light, you may wish to carry this protection with you on an everyday basis, without the use of ritual. To do this, simply visualize or imagine the Circle of Protection surrounding you. Imagine this as a bubble of clear or golden Light surrounding you and going with you everywhere you go. Take time to do this visualization every morning before leaving your home. Put the bubble around your home as well, around your car, and around your place of work. Renew the bubble of Light, your Circle of Protection, as frequently as you can remember to do it. Use this shielding as a way of life. It's another step in the total protection of your energy and your dedication to the Light.

The reconnection of your DNA and your formal dedication to the Light put you on a path of spiritual evolution. They are the beginning of a new, different life. If the changes happen too rapidly for comfort, go to the Lords of Karma and Divine Director and ask them for help integrating the energies and changes. There may be times when the process seems like a roller coaster ride. Understand that everyone on a spiritual path has undergone this process, which is an initiation in itself. Though it may seem overwhelming at times, nothing will harm you. Trust in the Light and the Goddess and know that you are becoming stronger and more whole, more fully filled with Light, with each passing day.

Dedicating yourself to the Light brings into your energy and your life more help than you ever knew existed. Rely on that help and learn to use it to ease your way. As your Light vibration increases, much that has harmed you in the past can no longer reach you, and your energy will be cleared of negative interference from the past. You will make many requests to the Lords of Karma and Divine Director to release this negative energy and you will become aware of it releasing. New types of negative interference may be drawn to your growing Light, but you will be protected and kept safe. While dedication is the beginning, the process of protection has only just begun. You will learn many more methods of protecting, clearing, and healing your energy, and increasing the raising of your Light vibration. These methods continue in the next chapter with processes to protect and shield your home.

4

PROTECTING YOUR HOME

A house or apartment that is under attack or filled with negative energy is a miserable place to live. The people who live there feel depressed, sleepless, even ill. Pets or children are agitated and aggressive, they misbehave, and they may even try to run away. They may refuse to enter the home, they may avoid or refuse to enter certain rooms or parts of rooms. Small animals like gerbils or caged birds may die. House plants wither and die, and there may be infestations of mice or fleas. Things break, leak, fall over, catch fire. The atmosphere is edgy, and no one feels safe, secure, or comfortable. People argue. People and pets would rather be anywhere else than at home and will find excuses to stay away as much as possible. It's not a good way to live.

In the recent two weeks, a leaky toilet cost me a $176 water bill plus $40 in repairs. A second toilet overflowed days later from a faulty water valve and then became stuffed. A sink began to leak. Next, the Christmas tree overturned, breaking over $100 in ornaments, some irreplaceable. A picture fell off the wall and the refrigerator heated up, requiring $150 in repairs plus spoiled food. When I finally found and passed the entity over, the ghost that wanted my attention, the bills and leaks stopped and both I and the ghost were much relieved. The means to pass-over ghosts and entities will be discussed later in this chapter.

Before my present home, I rented a house for a year that required two to three repair people a week, and I never felt comfortable living in it. None of the systems worked for more than a few days at a time without something breaking or going wrong. The wiring was ungrounded and unsafe and I couldn't wait to move. A week before I did, the automatic garage door disengaged from its track and fell from the garage roof, missing me by inches. The house had what I thought was a pine tree deva that talked to me and teased my dogs. Kali in particular was agitated by it, and explained some of her misbehavior by saying that the pine tree told her to do it. The "deva" proved to be a negative elemental and quite malevolent. I was told it was not safe for me to try to clear it, but that it would be removed after I left. By appealing to my Guardian Angels and the Lords of Karma, I made very sure it did not follow me to my new home.

In another rental, I woke almost nightly with nightmares of a neighbor, an elderly woman, who seemed to be in my bedroom shaking me awake and yelling at me. She was mentally disturbed. She stood outside my house almost daily, threatening me with the police, throwing bread and lunchmeat into my yard for the dogs, and telling me that one of my dogs "had evil in her." When she did call the police for no apparent reason, they told me that she "wasn't right" and called them often. I avoided her, but her nighttime visits disturbed my sleep. She was astral projecting and I didn't want her in my house. The protection dome ritual given later in this chapter stopped her visits, without harming her in any way. She became very angry when I did it.

A protected home feels entirely different. People and pets want to be there and they flourish, free to live in any room. Animals and children behave and no one argues; everyone is at peace and gets along. House plants bloom. There are no strange noises, visits, breakage, no pest infestations. Appliances and systems operate smoothly with minor need for repairs. Sleep is peaceful and undisturbed, without restlessness, nightmares, or insomnia. Privacy is secure. Everyone feels safe, rested, and well, viewing home as a refuge from the world. Everyone who enters feels protected and is protected from disturbance and harm. This is what a home is meant to be.

It doesn't matter whether you rent or own your home, or whether it is an apartment, room, house, or even a temporary motel room or dormitory. Your home is anywhere you sleep, and anywhere you do meditation or energy work. For your life and work to be protected, your home must be safe. Consider your home to be an outer shell or layer to your personal aura, surrounding it and forming a defense against the negative dark. For this to be so, your home must be as protected and filled with Light as your aura is. To neglect this is to leave you open to all sorts of disturbance and attack, all sorts of interference with your way of life. To fully protect your home you have to more fully protect your energy and your Light.

It is important to make your home a sacred space. This means not only your altar and meditation room, but the whole house, along with its surrounding grounds, garage, and garden. Consider your car as a part of your home, too, as well as your place of work away from home. These are all places where you spend your time and entrust your body and your energy. The room where you meditate or do energy work, or work with the Lords of Karma and Divine Director should be especially protected and kept especially sacred. As you are most energetically vulnerable when you sleep, your bedroom should also be made fully sacred and safe. These protections are separate from and along with your personal protection. Your home is a place for the Light and the Goddess to enter; make it safe for Her to do so.

These protections, however, need to be crafted carefully. A wall that shuts everything out, or all psychic energy out, is a mistake. You want shielding from negative interference and evil, but do not want to live inside a bell jar. When no energy can enter a space, the space dies very quickly, and these spaces are stifling and totally uncomfortable to live in. You do not want to live alone in a fort behind high walls and cut off from energy, Light, and life. You want as much admittance of the Light to your home as possible and of your helpers and healers of the Light. You also want protections that allow energy inside to leave, so that what you clear can be moved out. If you remove negative energy from your home it must be allowed to leave. To prevent that makes your home's energy quite toxic very rapidly.

So the question is how to create protection and shielding for your home that allows the Light in, prevents negative interference and evil from entering, and removes all negative energies from within. The energy of your home must breathe—breathe in Light and breathe out and release all unwanted energies. It must let in positive energy and Light Be-ings, while removing and keeping out all negative energies and entities that are disruptive or harmful. You must be protected from attack and from others' negative emotions but open to healing, help, growth, and love. All house (and personal) protections must be two way and fluid, they cannot be static and impermeable. The protections of this chapter, and this book, are designed to meet these needs.

Start at the physical level, the simplest beginning. As silly as it sounds, start with housecleaning. Throw away all objects and things that are broken, used up, or no longer useful. Clean your drawers and closets, again removing or giving away what no longer fits or you no longer need. To sort and straighten out your drawers and your home both clears and changes your life.

Pay attention to the objects that surround you. If any come from people whose energy you don't want in your life, either clear the objects' energy thoroughly or give them away. Clear them by placing them in salt for a week, washing them in the clothes washer or dishwasher, or filling them with Reiki. Use the Sei-Hei-Kei. You may go to the Lords of Karma and Divine Director to change the energy in these objects. Often it is best to simply remove them from your environment completely. Clean your refrigerator and food cupboard, too.

When I moved to Florida ten years ago I was very poor. I brought with me all the furniture I had, most of it quite shabby, and many knick-knacks and glass ornaments collected over the years, some going back to childhood. My childhood and adult-hood until then had not been happy and when I moved I was determined to leave my old life behind. It never occurred to me to leave the physical objects behind and I could not afford to replace them. In my new city, I discovered used furniture stores and for very small amounts of money began replacing the least attractive of my furniture. I bought many small objects in these stores, as well—glass figurines, quilts, stuffed toys, linens.

Over a period of three years I replaced every piece of furniture I had moved with, even down to the bookshelves that rusted in the Florida damp and heat. I did not do it intentionally, but kept finding better things to replace the old ones. I found these things one by one, at times when I could afford them, and the pieces were always attractive, matched my decor, and were incredibly inexpensive. I continued with the small objects—dishes, silverware, kitchen items, wall pictures, drapes, even jewelry. I gained weight and all my clothing changed, too.

Only when I had replaced nearly everything I had moved to Florida with did I realize what I was doing. By this time I was at the very end of the process and I continued it to completion.

Had I felt the need in the beginning for total change, the idea would have seemed overwhelming and financially impossible. Nevertheless it happened. All that remained of my old life was a few treasured objects given to me by my dead grandmother, some photographs, and my books. I changed my whole life and now have the new life I wanted.

Once you have sorted your belongings and removed those with bad memories or those that came from people you do not wish part of your surroundings, do a thorough housecleaning. Dust, wash curtains, do laundry, mop floors, put things away. Never leave dirty dishes overnight in the sink; besides drawing insects they negatively effect the energetics of your home. Take all the crystals and gemstones in your home, and your gemstone jewelry, and place them in salt water or dry sea salt. Include the jewelry you are wearing. If you have not done this in a long time they can take as long as a week to clear, but most items clear in twenty minutes to an hour. Use a pendulum to check when they are finished, but leave each item in salt until it is fully cleared.

Place a saucer full of salt in each of the four corners of your home, North, South, East, and West, plus a saucer in the Center. You may do this both indoors and out. If you feel you need to, place small bowls or saucers of salt on the windowsills. A couple of tablespoonsful of salt is enough in each saucer or bowl. Leave these in place for a week, after which time you may choose to remove them or replace them with fresh salt. Do not reuse, and never eat, salt that has been used for the clearing of crystals, objects, or rooms. Flush used salt down the toilet.

After the salt is in place, put a handful of dried sage or cedar (or the combination of the two) in a cast iron pot, frying pan, abalone shell, or large incense burner and light it with a match. Use these herbs specifically; they are available and inexpensive in health food and metaphysical stores. Sage and cedar catch fire slowly, but once they do they can spark, so be careful in the handling. Flying sparks can damage your carpets and furniture and may be a fire hazard—keep an eye on them. As the sage and cedar burns it makes a cloud of wonderful-smelling smoke that is used to dispel negative energies in places and on people.

Using your hand or a feather to direct the smoke, first breathe it, then fan the smoke over your body, front and back, including around your head, hands, and feet. Very few people are truly allergic to the smoke of organic herbs. All negative energies sticking to the surface of your aura will leave. This is called smudging. You will next smudge all the rooms of your home. You may smudge your pets as well, but don't overwhelm them with the smoke. Their sense of smell is much stronger than ours. Take the pan of smoking herbs through each room, fanning smoke through the room, and around each doorway and window frame. Be sure to smudge your altar and your crystals and sacred objects.

Move through your rooms in a counterclockwise direction for the clearing of negative energy. Move counterclockwise through your home or apartment and counterclockwise through each room. Smudge each room thoroughly, not forgetting the bathroom, garage, and kitchen,. Smudge around and inside your car, as well. If you have fire alarms, you may wish to place them outdoors while you are smudging and until the smoke clears. Once you are done smudging, you may wish to open windows and air the rooms. Let the sunlight in. While smudging and moving through the rooms, state: "Only the Light may enter here, all that is not of the Light must leave." Repeat this smudging monthly or whenever you feel you need to do it. If there has been an argument or negative person or event in your home, you can clear the energy by smudging. If you can also do this process where you work, so much the better.

When your house is thoroughly cleared, it's time to install the permanent dynamic shielding mentioned earlier, and to do a ritual to activate it. For this you will need seven, nine, or eleven pieces of one-eighth-inch copper tubing, each piece about five inches long. This is available cheaply at hardware stores. Ask the store to cut the pieces for you. Take these pieces outdoors and place them in a circle around the outside perimeter of your yard or grounds. Include your car and driveway within the circle. Hammer the pieces of copper into the ground, so that they don't stick up, and so no one can be hurt on them or remove them. Once they are in, you won't see them anymore, and you don't need to remember where they are. At the four directions of this circle, you may optionally bury a clear quartz crystal—it can be an imperfect garden-quality one.

Now go back indoors and enter your meditation space. Light your altar candle and cast a Circle of Protection as in the last chapter. Call upon the Guardians of the Four Directions, plus the Center, Above and Below. Call upon your Guardian Angel, and ask for the Guardian Angels of your home and car. Ask for the presence of the Lords of Karma and Divine Director and of any other Be-ings of the Light that you wish. When you visualize the Casting of your Circle, visualize it following the path of your copper rods and encircling your home. Do this moving clockwise, this time to create rather than to clear.

Visualize a circle of blue light following the pathway of the copper rods, encircling your home and its perimeters. Make the circle three-dimensional, turning the vision into a blue light dome that covers your home like a bowl. Make the bowl into a spherical ball by visualizing it extending under your home and grounds, as well. When you have completed this, you and your home will be inside a sphere of blue light that extends around, over, and under your home. The sphere includes your garden, garage, and car out to the perimeters of your property. You, your family, and your pets, are inside the home within the sphere.

Ask to speak with the Lords of Karma and Divine Director, your Guardian Angels, and the Guardian Angels of your house. Your first request is that your home and all in it (everything and everyone) be dedicated fully to the Light. Include you, your family, your pets, yard, and car, and all the objects that you own. Do this especially with your crystals, as they are important healing tools that transmit energy to you and your surroundings. Take this through the Lords of Karma process. Next ask that all negative and harmful energies be removed forever from all of these, and that they be protected totally from all negative energies and evil. This is the second Lords of Karma process and request. Then ask that your home and all in it be filled continually with so much Light that no evil or negativity can enter, remain, or exist there. Do the full Lords of Karma process again. Finally, ask for your home and all in it to be sealed unto the Light and unto protection forever.

Now ask that your protection dome be activated and the activation sealed. You must specify that the dome is to admit the Light and the positive dark, and all sources of the Light and the Goddess. It is to reject the negative dark and all negative energies, all negative interference and all that is evil. Also specify that the dome and your home be self-clearing, that any negative energies from within must be removed and given a way to leave harmlessly. Specify that all who come into your home be protected, healed, and cleared, and that only those of the Light or without harm be permitted to enter. (You may be surprised and relieved at who *doesn't* come around anymore!) Use this wording to make your request and when you have made it, go through another Lords of Karma and Divine Director process. Ask for the presence and help of your Guardian Angels and the

Guardian Angels of your house to keep you safe and your home safe, wherever you may live, forever. For your last process, ask for the blessing of the Light and the Goddess for you, your home, and all who live there.

At this point your dome will turn into a wall of Light and there may be a great deal of activity. You may psychically perceive almost a tornado of moving energy sweeping through your home and around it. Many of the things being swept away in that tornado will not be positive. Remain in your Cast Circle and protected space while the activity continues, or until you are told that you may open the Circle. When you are told to do so, thank the Lords of Karma and Divine Director, your Guardian Angels, and the Guardian Angels of your home. Thank and release the Guardians of the Four Directions, the Center, Above and Below. Declare that: "This Circle is open but unbroken. Merry meet and merry part, and merry meet again. Blessed Be." Blow out your candles. You may now leave your altar and meditation space.

This process will remove all negativity, and prevent most or all negative entities from entering. You may need to repeat the ritual occasionally, but it will usually last for years in the same house. No new copper rods will be required, unless you move to a new house or apartment, upon which the process needs to be redone. Despite the power of this dome, however, ghosts or entities may still come into your home for help. Since they are more lost than harmful, the shielding may not prevent them from entering, though they still can be disruptive. Some psychics have a karmic contract for helping discarnate entities pass over, and if you are one of them, those in need will find you. That an entity is not alive does not automatically make it evil. If grandma was a wonderful person in life, she will not be an evil ghost. (Those who are evil will be kept out by the dome.) Most such entities are harmless.

By "entity" I mean the spirit or presence of a person or animal who was once alive but is no longer living. I prefer this term to "ghost," the popular term for the same thing. Similar energy that is *not* from a once-alive person or animal is called an "attachment," and has the potential for greater harm. The intrusive presence of someone who is still living is called an "astral shade," "astral fetch," or "astral presence." This is the result of conscious or unconscious astral projection. My former nasty neighbor was an astral presence. These will be filtered out by your protection dome and will not be able to enter your home.

You will know that an entity is in your house by the disruption it causes. There may be cold or heavy spots in the house, or rooms which your pets refuse to enter or lie down in. You too may find yourself avoiding the room or corner of a room that holds this negative energy. Dogs and cats easily see these entities and may spend their time watching them, fascinated. They are rarely frightened of them, but they seem to be watching air, or playing with something unseen, especially if the entity was once a cat, dog, or child. Pets that have died will sometimes visit in this way. Your living pets will be glad to greet and play with an old friend.

Noises in the night or when things are quiet, possibly footsteps, bumps, or sounds of someone moving around when no one is there are all signs of an entity in the house. There may be voices or laughter, floating faces or balls of light, footprints, slime marks, or strange odors. Doors slam and appliances or lights may turn on and off. Pictures fall off the walls. (Entities drop pictures frequently in my house and while they seldom are damaged, the noise definitely gets my attention.) Glass objects can fall off their shelves for no explainable reason and sometimes they break. Things move out of place from where I've put them, or appear and disappear. There may be a run of broken household appliances or plumbing that needs to be repaired.

When you enter a room you may feel you are not alone or that someone has just left or has just moved out of your range of vision. You may wake with nightmares or feeling a weight on your chest, or wake with strange bruises. You may feel agitated, nervous, and exhausted and have trouble sleeping. If the entity was depressed when it died, you may also feel depressed. You may simply feel uneasy, that something is not right.

Who are they and why are they there? These entities or ghosts are the spirits of people or animals that have died. They are usually attached to houses where they once lived, or attracted to people with whom they had deep emotional connections in their lifetimes. These connections may be of love, or of lust, hate, or revenge. They may have died suddenly and may not be aware they are dead. Because they think they are alive or have refused to leave Earth for some reason, they remain on a dimension close to the earthplane in a not-dead and not-living state. They may be trapped in this way, unable to be alive and unable to pass over for a very long time. When they appear in your home—and it is usually places rather than people that they come to—it is because they are in need of help.

It is a common experience for someone dying to visit a loved one as they leave. The person they contact thinks of them, dreams of them, or wakes suddenly knowing that the person has gone. This has happened to me twice, once when my grandmother died. She came to me during the night at the same moment she passed over. Sometimes, however, the person dies suddenly—perhaps of a heart attack—and doesn't realize she is dead. She comes to visit her loved one and then stays. More often her spirit will return to the home she lived in at the time of her death, especially if she has spent much of her life there. Usually the person's angels and guides will find her and lead her to where she is supposed to go. Occasionally this doesn't happen, however, or the person refuses to go with their angels to complete their passing.

Such spirits can remain in a house for centuries, and most old houses have at least one of them. Usually they do no harm, they just want to go on "living" where they have always lived. They can be very helpful, like the entity I once knew that helped to maintain what used to be her garden for (and with) the living woman who now owns her house. They can stay to protect a child or a mate, or to harass someone they hated. An entity named Clara became the helpful resident of a healing center when the center moved into what had once been her home. Clara refused to pass over and became quite angry with me when I tried to send her. She wanted to stay and I agreed to let her, but I showed her how to leave if she wished to.

She woke the owner of the center up one night, showing her a candle left burning in an upstairs room. In the morning the candle was still burning but all was well; Clara had kept it safe. When the healing center closed and moved from the building, Clara chose to pass over. All who felt her presence in the center knew Clara for a friend.

Spirits who do not pass fully over are in a state of limbo. They cannot complete their death process, cannot receive the healing that comes to souls after death, and cannot reincarnate. If they became confused and rejected or missed their final passage, they may remain in limbo for a very long time. Entities who are ready to leave but don't know how to do so can be drawn to the homes of people who have the ability to help them. They may show up in your living room, crashing pictures, ringing bells, or teasing your dog to get your attention. When you know they are there, it is your job to complete their passing from life to death.

Once you are aware of a discarnate presence, it is best to find out what you are dealing with. I use a pendulum or meditation to ask these questions: Is this an entity? Is it human? Or an animal? Is it nonhuman? Is it harmful? Does it want help? Does it need to pass over? Does it know that it's dead? Is it male or female? Is there anything else I need to know about it? If you are told something doesn't need to pass over, ask if it needs to pass *under*. Some attachments and elementals, both nonhuman spirits, need to be passed under to the Fire of Life at the Center of the Earth. Their energy will be purified and recycled there. Human or animal spirits that have died, however, come to you to be passed over.

There are a couple of ways that you can do this. I generally ask the Lords of Karma to send who is needed to help the spirit, by taking it where it needs to go. Divine Director is not required for this, as we are dealing with an Earth lifetime. You can also ask your Guardian Angel and/or the entity's Guardian Angel to come and take it over. Or ask for some guide, relative, or a religious figure the person can trust to do the job. If the spirit resists leaving, you may have to tell it that it has died and insist that it leave. If it becomes threatening, ask your Guardian Angel for help. The entity can make some disturbance in your home, but it can do no real harm.

I like to psychically watch an entity pass over, just to make sure it has really gone. In the meditative state, ask to watch it pass. What I'm shown is an open doorway of golden light. The angel carries or leads the entity through the doorway, and once they have both gone through the door, it closes and is barred. Occasionally the door doesn't close or these spirits return, and the disturbances start all over again. Check to make sure they are gone and will stay gone. If they return, do the process again, this time asking the Lords of Karma that they not be permitted to come back. Some entities refuse to believe they are dead, are afraid that if they pass over they will be punished, or they really don't want to leave the house or the people they have stayed for. Reassure them that there is no punishment, they will be welcomed and healed. When an entity haunts a person's energy, rather than a house or building, the situation is called a possession. This is more serious and will be discussed in Chapter 9.

One other kind of home invasion bears mentioning here, that of fleas, ticks, ants, mice, larger wildlife, or other natural pests. I have found in Florida that any home or yard infested in a serious way with fire ants is also a home that is under psychic attack. Fire ants are biting red ants that can live in colonies of thousands. Significant numbers of these can kill a small pet or infant and harm a child, and their bite can cause serious illness in many adults. Inexplicable infestations of other insects, like fleas or ticks, or of undesirable small animals like rats or mice can also be an indication that the house is being attacked, though this is not always the case. Occasionally larger wildlife like raccoons will move into the rafters or garage of a house. They are usually just looking for a home and like the energy of yours. There are several things you can do.

First of all, the dome of Light will protect and clear your house of psychic attacks and once this is done you will find the insect infestations clear up by normal earthplane means. You can also ask for help. First go to the Lords of Karma and Divine Director and ask them to end the infestation *at the source* and remove the offending creatures. This will end the overrun of bugs or mice, and also the negative energy they are drawn to. If you are given further instructions, follow them.

Next, also in meditation, ask to speak to the Overlighting Deva of (let's say) fire ants. Tell the Deva that her people are where they are not welcome and that they must leave. Tell the Deva that you will have to exterminate them if they remain. Offer her a place for the ants to go, an uninhabited place, where you will not bother them, where they will not harm anyone, and where they can nest undisturbed. This can be an open lot, or woods far away—show her a picture. If you can engage the Deva's help, the ants will leave. (Ants tend to be belligerent, however, and the Lords of Karma are your best bet.)

In the case of a family of raccoons or squirrels in your attic, be flattered that they like your home's energy. However, you don't have to let them stay there. Again, first go to the Lords of Karma and Divine Director, asking that the animals be moved to a more positive place. Ask for the Overlighting Deva of raccoons or squirrels and request her help in finding the family a better place to live. You might also psychically contact the mother raccoon, telling her that she must find her family a new home. If you feel it is necessary to forcibly remove the animals, use a Havahart trap that doesn't kill or maim and take them safely to a wild place, at least five miles away. By the methods above, however, they will usually leave on their own and you will not need to interfere.

Be aware of the difference between harmless wildlife and an infestation of harmful pests. An overrun of rats or fire ants is harmful and may emerge from negative energies that are unnatural; a family of raccoons is not. Do not hesitate to ask the Lords of Karma and Divine Director for help with such nuisances. When the invasion seems unnatural, do not hesitate to look deeper than the insects or the animals themselves. Negative energy sent to harm you or your home can appear in this way. More than once I have cleared myself thoroughly of attacking energies, and when the negativity continued discovered that the source was attacking me by affecting my home. Make sure your home, family, and animals are protected.

Make sure that your car is also fully protected. Whatever house protection processes you do should always include your car. When you create the protection dome, make sure your car is inside it. When you smudge your house, smudge your car. Like your home, your car is an extension of your energy. If it is interfered with you may have a poorly running vehicle that is an expensive nuisance or even a dangerous accident. Individual people's negative emotions and malice toward you can by conscious or unconscious intent affect your home or car. Negative energy can be deliberately sent to harm you either directly or through attacking your home, car, garden, pets, or even your children or family members. The negative mass consciousness of the planet that makes the Earth a negative place can also make your home a negative place. You can protect yourself against such things with the methods in this chapter, by simply being aware that such things are possible, and with reliance on the Light.

5

DAILY PROTECTION

Now that you have dedicated yourself to the Light and protected your home, it is time to discuss some ways to protect your daily activities in the world. The focus here is more on the minor negativities that seem to stick to your aura than on serious or deliberate negative interference or psychic attacks. While nothing terribly dangerous may be going on, the daily grind can get you down. An aura repeatedly filled with Light repels much of this energy, unless the aura itself has been previously damaged. A useful request to the Lords of Karma and Divine Director is to ask to heal your aura of all damage from Earth and all other planets, through all lifetimes and between them, and including the present lifetime. You may be surprised at what you see if they show you visual pictures.

Your aura may show blotches and tears, smeared patches, trailing shreds of energy, dimmed or muddied colors, even rips, holes, and bald spots. Ask the Lords of Karma for complete healing for all of these, through all the levels, components, and systems of your Be-ing. Ask to heal them at the source, and from all sources of the damage. While some of this damage can be from negative interference, it is usually only the wear and tear of this and many other incarnations and between-incarnation states. We have all been around the block too many times.

Damage occurs in the aura from shock, pain, negative emotional states, physical injury, and mental aberrations. Every time you suffer something physically, emotionally, mentally, or spiritually, your aura is affected. If these damages are not fully healed in the lifetime in which they occur, they return in the next lifetime. If they are not healed then, they return again. The longer it takes to heal them, the deeper into your energy the damage moves, becoming core soul damage that is difficult to heal.

Ask the Lords of Karma and Divine Director for complete core soul healing. This is an important request and goes a long way to healing auric damage. It will not happen overnight, but over a period of many months. The request to clear, heal, reconnect, and activate the full complement of your DNA also provides for core soul and aura healing. As your DNA heals, your aura heals. Your core soul heals eventually. The more of the Radiance of the Light you ask to run through your energy, the more healing takes place as well.

These are the things to be aware of. Repeat the request to be filled with the Radiance of the Light often. Ask that the Light totally heal you of all aura and core soul damage.

Remember to cast your personal Circle of Protection as often as you can think of doing it. Request a bubble of Light to surround and protect you. This bubble is a copy of the dome that surrounds your home. It is a full sphere, reaching over your head and under your feet, surrounding you on all sides as well as above and below you. Consider it an extension of the ritually Cast Circle. If you can quickly Cast a formal Circle, asking for the protection of the Lords of Karma and Divine Director, your Guardian Angel, and the Guardians of the Directions, so much the better. You may not realize it, but the Guardians of the Four Directions, plus the Center, Above and Below are parts of your Oversoul. They are living Be-ings of the Light. If you see them psychically, they may appear as protecting dragons or as figures resembling the Oscar award. They incarnate with you for the purpose of protecting you, but may only enter your energy if you invite them. Remember to do so often.

Use the Cast Circle of Light every morning upon rising before you leave your protected home. Carry it with you into your workplace, remembering to charge and reactivate it often. To do this, you only need to think about it. Visualize the sphere or bubble and make it brighter. Think about your Guardian Angel and the Guardians of the Directions while asking them for and thanking them for their help. When entering a crowded place or public transportation, think of them again. Think of them before driving to protect you on the road. When involved in a situation that is unpleasant or negative or stressful in any way, think of them again. Visualize the sphere of Light, your personal Cast Circle, and visualize the Radiance of the Light inside it filling, clearing, and healing you.

There is no need to do a formal ritual to accomplish this. Once you understand what a Circle of Protection means and once you have created it, you can think it into Be-ing in an instant. When you do this often enough, it becomes a part of your aura and your energy, and eventually the Cast Circle is always there. This is a desirable goal, because once it happens you are continuously protected and filled with healing Light. As in every other aspect of psychic and protection work, your thoughts direct your energy. Only thinking about the Circle creates it and puts you inside it to be fully protected.

When you are within the Circle, nothing that is negative can affect or harm you. No matter what workday pressure, stress, or negative emotions may appear outside the Circle, inside it you are calm and impervious to it. This is something to work for. This is also a result of asking to raise your energy vibration beyond the effects of mass consciousness negativity. You do not buy into the hopelessness or the violence, you do not buy into the anger or the rage or the greed. No matter who is sending it toward you or emitting it from their energy, it has no effect on you at all. Your own calmness and Light remain intact.

When you achieve this state in yourself, you also affect others and help others achieve it. You need do nothing to cause this, it will simply happen. As your Light increases, it helps to heal the energy of those around you. As your vibration raises, it helps to raise others'. In the concept of critical mass, when the Light raises in enough individuals, it raises for everyone, and the planet is also raised. Each increase of Light in each individual helps other individuals, and eventually helps everyone and the Earth. While most people are taught to reach out to others, healing begins with you. Until you can bring Light to yourself, you cannot bring it to anyone else. But once you do bring it to yourself, you have the ability to heal the world.

It is most important to protect yourself in daily life from negative emotions, both yours and others'. Your own stress, anger, worry, and fear can fill your energy, preventing Light from flowing in and preventing help from reaching you. Try to keep an attitude of relaxed peace in everything you do. Nightly meditation will help you achieve this. Repeatedly ask in these meditations that your aura be filled with Light. Doing this will help keep you calm and clear. Other people's emotions bombard your aura every day at all times, though they do not intend to harm you. You must protect yourself from them.

Energy travels like ultrasound. It makes waves that move through everything in its path, turning what they touch into what they are. If the wave is of fear, you begin to feel fear, having no idea who or what that fear comes from or that the fear is not your own. Thought is energy and travels in this way, as well.

We are first influenced by emotions, and then by others' thoughts. We may have no idea that we are being influenced. If you have ever entered a room where someone is depressed and left that room feeling depressed, you have experienced this. It happens continually everyday.

Protecting yourself from the negative mass consciousness of the planet goes a long way toward protecting you from others' negative emotions and thoughts. So does clearing these negative thoughtforms from your own Mind Grid. These processes, along with the sphere of Light, help to place you above the pain you walk through each day. When you and your aura are strong and you have healed enough of the mass consciousness in yourself, it will be time for you to help to heal others. In the meantime, be aware of what the energy waves of the planet do to your energy and others' energy and try to keep above it.

If there are particularly negative people in your life, or people directing negative emotions specifically at you, there is more to be done. You must reinforce your Circle of Light frequently and fill yourself with Light constantly. Ask the Lords of Karma and Divine Director to make these protections continuous and to increase their Light and effectiveness to whatever you need to protect you. Someone else's jealousy, envy, or animosity can do harm, even if that person is not deliberately directing these emotions to attack you. Just that they feel them—and feel them about you—is enough. If they are deliberately attacking you with them, even more protection is needed. If you know who this person is, go to the Lords of Karma and Divine Director and ask them to protect you from their negativity.

You may also ask to heal your karma with this person, and to heal the source of their dislike of you. It may not be from this lifetime or even from a lifetime on Earth. You may ask for karmic severance with them if the situation is severe, and if the

Lords of Karma agree to its necessity. If you wish to end all interaction with the person, ask to cancel all karma and all karmic contracts with them from Earth and all planets, from all lifetimes and between all lifetimes. Do this only with the Lords of Karma and Divine Director's permission. You will end all contact with the person almost immediately, so think about it before you request it. If that person is your boss, you may lose your job. If he is your ex-husband, you may lose your child support or alimony. When in doubt, ask the Lords of Karma and Divine Director what is correct to ask for. Often just asking for karmic healing of the relationship and situation are enough.

Some mention of ethics is appropriate here. We are working to achieve greater Light and greater connection to Goddess. This cannot be done by acting in negative or unethical ways toward others for whatever reason. There is always an ethical way to handle any situation. Any request to the Lords of Karma and Divine Director is a request for yourself, not a request to "do something" to someone else. You may protect your energy with Light, but you may not use your energy to return negativity or to attack anyone. This is so no matter how bad the situation or the person may seem or be. There is always an ethical way. When you send negative energy you become it, and that is the last thing you wish ever to do.

You must not in any way violate another's free will or ability to make their own choices or choose their own destiny. That includes not violating others' ability to make their own mistakes, or what you think is a mistake, and to learn from them. You cannot prevent someone from speaking against you, acting against you, or having negative emotions regarding you. You can, however, protect yourself from receiving that energy. How someone chooses to act is their free will. Your freedom is in choosing what you will or won't accept.

You may not manipulate another's choices. The classic example of this is the love spell, where someone is coerced into becoming your mate. These relationships seldom work out, and the person asking for it usually gets something different from what was expected. Instead of forcing someone to love you, ask for your own true mate. The right person will be drawn to you, and you will find happiness together. The person who comes to you of their own free will make a far better relationship than someone who is manipulated into it. The first relationship will last, the second will prove to be abusive or otherwise unhappy. If that coerced person was meant to be your mate, he or she would have come to you freely. If they do not, it was not meant to be.

This is also true in a healing situation, as difficult as that can be. Someone you love is suffering and you know they can be helped—by psychic healing, karmic work, or even something from the medical system. But the person with the dis-ease refuses. Ethically, you must accept their choice. You cannot force them to receive what will heal them, even if you think it's for their own good. To insist is to violate that person's freedom and free will, something which must never be done for any reason. The person refusing help may have very good reasons for doing so. It may be her time to die, and she is ready to leave. She may have fulfilled her karmic agreements for this lifetime.

It may be that the healing is to happen in another way and at another time, and forcing it prevents some greater good. It may also be that the person has something to learn from her dis-ease and is not ready to heal it now or never will be. She may have a karmic contract with the dis-ease that must be fulfilled. Just as you may not send negative energy to anyone, you may not violate anyone's choice to refuse positive or healing energy.

When you send negative energy or manipulate free will, you remove yourself from the Light and from the Goddess. You also incur karma that must be resolved, either instantly or later. Instant resolution is much more merciful than carrying these debts into other lifetimes, but it's better not to incur such debts at all. When in doubt, ask the Lords of Karma what is ethical and what to do. When in doubt, fill yourself with Light and ask for healing and resolution for yourself and for the situation. Protect yourself with Light, and never think, send, or intend harm or negativity toward anyone, not even toward your worst enemy. Never go against others' choices, even for their own good. This is absolutely essential. By remaining in the Light, you allow the Lords of Karma and the Light and the Goddess to deal with the situation properly and for the highest good of all. Remember that the other person also has karma and is accountable for their deeds and actions. Let the Light deal with that person who is harming you. "The wheels of the gods grind slowly, but they grind exceedingly fine."

A special word about protecting healers is appropriate at this time. Healers are usually empaths, which means that they care about other people so much that they feel and experience their pain. They may care and feel so much that they take others' pain into themselves, consciously or not. Some healers are actually taught to do this, or think that it's the only way to do healing. There is no need for this and it can cause harm to the healer without benefit to the person being healed. Negative energy need not be directed toward or taken through your own energy to help others. There are a multitude of other ways to remove others' pain. There are many other places to send sickness during healing work, places that end the negativity harmlessly and forever.

If you are a healer or wish to be, the first thing to do is to take Reiki. This is the beginning of all healing methods and will enhance your healer's abilities no matter what methods you wish to use. If you are an empath who takes others' pain into yourself when you do healing, Reiki I is usually enough to stop you from doing so. By the time you have reached Reiki III you will be able to deal with any type of sickness or dis-ease, any type of negativity that can be cleared in a healing session, without it affecting you or causing you harm. As this planet grows, evolves, and clears, more and more energy workers and healers are needed. By refusing to accept the negativity you clear from others, you become a stronger and more effective healer, more able to meet the planet's needs.

During a healing session, make use of the Lords of Karma, Divine Director, and your Guardian Angel (by now you should know your angel's name). Ask for their presence and help at the start of every healing session. If the person receiving the healing releases a dis-ease, harmful emotion, or past life situation, an attachment, possession, or energy from negative interference, or attacks, call upon them to help. If you don't understand what you are seeing, ask your Guardian Angel to both protect you from it and show you what to do with it. With this-life or past life situations to heal or be released, ask for the help of the Lords of Karma and Divine Director. If your client is receptive, teach her how to work with them, as well.

If you pull something negative from someone's energy, ask your Guardian Angel to take it away. Use the words "annihilate, extinguish, uncreate, and obliterate it forever," if that is what is needed. Place it in a flame to purify and clear it, or call upon the Angels of Blue Lightning to deal with it. Call upon Archangel Michael to defeat all attacking and evil energies; he is a major protector of this planet. Archangel Ashtar deals with negativity from other planets that attack Earth or Earth Be-ings. Whatever the source of the negativity, make very sure that it is truly gone before you relax your attention. If you don't, it may come back again. If you send an attachment to the Fire of Life at the Center of the Earth, follow its progress psychically until you know it has reached that place, and the sacred white flames have consumed it. Otherwise that attachment may return and cause more harm, and must be removed again.

Whether you encounter negative energies or painful past lives in your healing work, ask the Lords of Karma and Divine Director to clear the situation *at the source*. This source may be in a beginning situation or event from this life or from other lifetimes. The source may or may not have originated on Earth. To clear a past life that appears in a healing is positive, but to clear its source is to heal it through all lifetimes forever. Dis-eases also have a source. Asking to heal the karma of the dis-ease at its source is the best way to end it. Also ask to cancel all karma and all karmic contracts with both the dis-ease and all sources of the dis-ease, from Earth and all planets, and between them, all lifetimes and between them.

If you are dealing with a physical dis-ease, or an emotional, mental, or spiritual one, ask the Lords of Karma and Divine Director to remove it from the person's DNA. Ask to heal the damaged section of DNA that is causing replication of the dis-ease, replacing any strands or components that must be changed for the replication to end. Ask to bring that section of the DNA and all the DNA back to its full purity and perfection, free of dis-ease, fully healed and regenerated. This is a good way to work with cancer, AIDS, or other life-threatening conditions. Ask also to cancel all karma and all karmic contracts with the dis-ease and with all sources of it. Again, this request should be for all lifetimes on Earth, and all other planets, and between them. It should also be through all the levels and components of the person's energy, through all dimensions, all connections, and all systems. Use these words in your requests and do the full Lords of Karma and Divine Director process.

When you complete your healing sessions, or come home from a day of energy bombardment at work or in a city environment, make an effort to clear yourself of all the negative energies and emotions you may have brought home. Such energies can stick to your aura, and if not brushed off, can reduce your vitality, create dis-ease, and inflict energy or aura damage. There are some simple ways to do this. One is to hold your dominant hand, palm open, over a bowl or saucer full of sea salt. While doing this, request that all that is negative in your energy enter the salt to be purified. Hold your hand over the salt until you feel the clearing. You will be aware of the energy shift. Then flush the salt down the toilet. Some people give such energies to the Earth, but I feel that the Earth has far too much negativity to handle already. You may send your negativity, however, to the Fire of Life at the core of the planet for purification and recycling.

The next way to clear yourself of negativity is to take a shower. You may take a half-cup of sea salt in a plastic container into the shower with you and use it for purification. To do this, first wet your body, then rub the salt over each of your chakras front and back. You may or may not wish to place salt on your Crown Chakra unless you are about to wash your hair. Do not place it on your genitals, as the salt will burn. When doing this, don't forget your hands and feet. Leave the salt on your body for a few moments, then rinse it off. Repeat the process for a total of three times, rinse off and take your normal shower. You will feel much refreshed at the end. It is best not to dress again in the clothes you came home in. Wash them before you wear them to clear the energies they are carrying.

Another way to clear yourself of negative energy is to take a cleansing bath containing a cup of sea salt and a cup of baking soda. Make the bath as hot and as full as is comfortable for you, and expect to stay in the water for at least half an hour. This is something to do about twice a month. You will not want to do it any more often than weekly. After about twenty minutes, you may suddenly feel ill or nauseous and the once clear water will turn black. Remain in the bath until the discomfort ends, it usually takes no more than five minutes. When you emerge from the bath you will feel weak and drained—but cleared of negativity. Dry yourself, then get into bed and allow yourself time to sweat. When this is finished, in less than an hour, you will be amazed at how good you will feel.

A further way to clear your energy and release any negative energy vibrations from your day is to do the smudging suggested in the last chapter. This time, however, smudge only yourself. Light the sage or cedar in a fireproof container and fan the smoke through your aura. Begin by breathing the smoke, which has a lovely fragrance, then fan it through your energy from head to foot on both the front and back of your body. Make sure to do your hands and feet, and to clear each of the chakras. The closest-to-physical kundalini chakras are located at the places you touched in the Self-Blessing ritual. A series of chakras exists on each of the many levels and bodies of your energy, but smudging only reaches the physical and emotional layers. These alone make a great difference, however, and can clear a majority of the energies you pick up in a normal day.

The next level up is your mind. Calm it by clearing it of all thoughts and concerns of your job. When you change your mind you also change your energy. Forget the stresses, problems, difficulties, and conflicts and leave them for your workday tomorrow. Leave them at the door to your home, and don't pick them up again until you leave again for work—if you must pick them up at all. Ask the Lords of Karma and Divine Director to clear and calm your mind and fill it with Light. Ask to release all negative thoughts, all problems, and all worries. Absolutely reject all worst case scenarios. If you must think about a difficulty, think of how it can best be resolved. When you give your worries to the Light the problems solve themselves. Make a conscious decision to have a positive mind, a mind that is free of negativity.

Changing your environment also changes your energy. Upon returning home, create an atmosphere and environment of the greatest peace, totally different from your workplace. If your home is protected by the methods of the previous chapter, this should be extremely easy to do. Take your salt shower or salt bath and put on soft and comfortable clothing. Play music that soothes your soul—New Age, classical, folk, blues, or jazz— nothing jarring, staccato, metallic, or irritating. Try a quiet background of nature sounds and whale song. Use soft lighting in your home, or candles and incense; use aromatherapy oils. Make a dinner of fresh foods. Read a good book. Do your meditations. Relax.

If you live or work in the city, it is good to find some time in your day or week to reconnect with nature. You can do this by having a pet or a garden, or even some potted plants in your home. Natural energy calms and relaxes. Animals will clear people of negativity, even of dis-eases and negative interference. People with animals live longer and have fewer heart attacks, strokes, and depression. Cats transmute most harmful energies easily. Dogs do this as well, but a dog may need help if you are constantly stressed or ill or if you come home daily filled with negativity you can't shake off. To help your pet, become calm. To help yourself, pet and love your animal. Both you and the pet will benefit, and the exchange is mutually healing. Walking a dog brings you back to the Earth and helps to ground you if you are agitated. Remember occasionally to hug a tree; it also will result in an exchange of energy that clears and grounds you.

Restrict your contact with television and the media and choose your movies and entertainments carefully. Today's media is a daily horror of disasters, mass deaths, violence, bombings, plane crashes, and greedy corporations and politicians. There is only so much of this you can take without being affected and weakened by it. It brings you full tilt against the negative mass consciousness you are trying to protect yourself against. Remember that though there is pain and suffering in the world, there is also joy. Remember that for every horror on the nightly news there are a great many blessings that never reach the screen. If you must have daily newscasts it is better to listen to them on the radio or read a newspaper than to watch them on TV. The information is bad enough without the pictures. It is also best to avoid newscasts just before sleep. They do little to promote sweet dreams.

I make it a policy to avoid bringing violence into my life. I will not go to violent movies, though that greatly restricts the movies available to me. It also greatly increases my enjoyment of the movies I choose to see. Years ago I made the decision not to have a television, again to reduce the violence in my direct environment. Violence perpetuates violence, and television is a primary source of the negativity of our planetary collective consciousness. Surrounded by violence, you become hardened to it, your aura becomes filled with it until no more can enter—and until nothing else can enter. I choose to keep my aura filled with Light, and refuse violence as a means of entertainment. A non-violent mind draws no violence. What you think and how you think is how you live.

A further way to heal and protect yourself and your aura from negative energy and negative interference is to help others. By your service to others and the Earth, you bring Light into your own energy and you also heal the Earth. Some people incarnated at this time of planetary crisis are bodhisattvas. This means that they have completed their requirement to reincarnate, but they choose not to do so for the purpose of helping others. Many bodhisattvas are incarnated on Earth at this time, though only some of them know who they are. If you are on the path of Ascension in this lifetime, as probably everyone reading this book is, you have achieved it in other lifetimes or on other planets. This makes you a bodhisattva. You are here on Earth now to help ascend the Earth, to raise its energy vibration so that all may be healed. This is no small goal or small task, and everyone is needed to complete it. The more people doing service, the sooner the task is done.

Spend some of your time, whatever time you can spare and in whatever way you can, helping others. This can be as simple as sending your outgrown clothes to a flood relief effort, or as complex as joining Vista or the Peace Corps. It can mean using your healing abilities to help a friend, or giving a little of your money to feed a child. Become a mentor to someone in your office, or a tutor for an inner city teenager, or help an elder do her weekly grocery shopping. It doesn't have to be much, and it doesn't have to cost much, but every little bit you do raises the energy of the planet and your own.

What you give out returns to you tenfold. Every help you offer also helps you. It may not sound like psychic protection to do this, but in the long run it is. Everything you do to raise your Light vibration, or the vibration of someone else or of the planet will help to heal and protect you. And someone you help may have information or healing or a helping hand that makes a crucial difference in a time of your own crisis or need. Take your focus off of your worries and your daily life and help someone. It will heal you in many ways.

The next chapter discusses ways to clear and fill your energy with Light.

6

ENERGY CLEARING

Part of the process of healing damage to your aura and energy system lies in keeping all components, bodies, chakras, and channels free flowing and clear. As Light is brought through you to flow through your aura, it flushes out things that need to be removed. These can be dis-eases, blockages, bits of old karma, negative energy of all types, residues, and even old ideas—all kinds of outworn energy. The process is similar to old skin cells flaking off when you wash your face. These leftovers need to be taken away for your energy systems to function optimally. The more energy clearing you can do, the more free flowing the Light. The more free flowing the Light, the more rapid the healing of aura damage and the removal of all negativity. The more free flowing the Light, the more you are protected from further energy damage, negativity, and harm.

While the terms "clearing," "cleansing," and "purification" are used frequently for these processes, please understand that no one's energy is "dirty." Traditional religions place a burden of guilt, sin, shame, and "uncleanliness" on humanity. This is simply not true. Neither people nor their energies are to be considered dirty or unclean, nor are the energies of animals or other life. Nor are our physical bodies "dirty" in any way, and that includes any of our physical functions, including sexuality and elimination. We are all Be-ings of the highest Light, created in total purity and perfection. Energy clearing means raising your Light vibration by removing from your aura and systems all out-worn energies and all energies that hold back your evolution and soul growth.

When you ask to be filled with Light, and particularly when you ask to be filled with Light continually, you are asking to raise your vibration. When you continually fill a bathtub with water it eventually overflows, unless there is an overfill drain near the top for the excess to run out. Energy clearing creates the overfill drain, and what goes down the drain is the lowest vibrational levels of your energy. The more these lowest levels funnel off down the drain, the clearer your energy becomes. As your average level of clarity rises, so does your total average vibrational level. This raising of the average overall vibrational level of your energy is called evolution.

In the concept of critical mass, when enough people raise their average overall vibrational level, it raises the level of the entire planet. What was once the lowest level has been funneled off down the overflow drain, so the lowest level rises. By raising the lowest level, you also make way for raising the highest possible level. As more and more people raise their energy vibrations, the Earth's vibration rises. As more and more people achieve Ascension, the raising of their energy to fifth-dimensional levels, the Earth will also reach Ascension as a whole. To achieve Ascension means to clear enough of your Earth karma so that you no longer are required to reincarnate. This involves raising your energy, and the planet's energy, from its original third-dimensional level to the fifth dimension. We are now at the fourth-dimensional level and rising rapidly. Beyond the fifth-dimensional level, karma no longer exists. By raising individual vibration, you clear your karma and your need to reincarnate, and raise the planet so that karma will eventually end on Earth for everyone.

Cleared energy also feels good. If you can imagine not washing your face for a week, imagine how good washing it at last would feel. This is so with your nonphysical energy and aura, as well. Unlike face washing, we have not been taught to clear and wash our energy systems. Some amount of clearing takes place automatically, but to do a full wash accelerates the process immensely, and with it your sense of well-being. When you are doing intensive psychic protection and energy work, it makes the process smoother and faster to request that your energy be kept cleared. Cleared energy is also protected energy, as clearing removes a lot of negativity that could harm you, negativity that slows your evolution. This basically is what negative interference does, it slows down your evolution and the raising of your vibration. When you keep your energy cleared, you wash out old interference, prevent new interference from gaining hold, and increase the speed of the raising of your vibration.

The Earth and all planetary systems have mechanisms for clearing negative and outmoded energies, too. On a physical level, these can be as dramatic as volcanoes and hurricanes or as simple and helpful as rain or a light cooling breeze. To move energy usually means to clear it; unmoving energy does not clear and becomes stagnant. Stagnation evokes the image of a swamp, something fetid and unhealthy. The term energy itself, however, means change. Moving, changing energy is energy in the process of clearing. By doing Lords of Karma work you promote changes in your life, because the processes cause your energy systems and components to move from stagnation to clearing, from negativity to Light. Though most people resist change, change is healthy. When the full clearing and full effects of the changes are complete, few people want to return

91

to where the process began. They know they are better off than they were before.

The planet is also in the process of clearing and changing, and raising her overall average vibration. Two new planetary grids have been recently brought into Be-ing, recent in the thousands of years' measure of planetary evolution. Grids are the electrical systems of the Earth; most planets have fourteen grids and Earth's current ten is being raised to fourteen. The grids resemble the latitude and longitude lines on a map, and the easiest to reach grid, the Earth Grid, contains the ley line system that dowsers are familiar with. The two newest grid structures are in the core of the Earth at the center of the planet, under rather than over it. These are the Well of Life at the Center of the Earth and the Fire of Life at the Center of the Earth.

The Well of Life is the life force of creation. Its keeper is Nada, Earth's creation Goddess and Great Mother. All life emerges from the Well of Life and all pure water sources originate there. Flower essences heal because they carry some essence or energy of the Well, which was also King Arthur's Holy Grail and Archangel Michael's Chalice of Healing and Regeneration. Water is the source of all Earth life and healing—the oceans, streams, rivers, and lakes. Without pure water we would die; without water we would not exist or be created at all. In the interplanetary war that damaged Earth's creation, the Well of Life at the Center of the Earth was attacked. Its purity was fouled and its flow reduced and blocked. We have all suffered from this reduction of our birthright life force, the reduction of our ability to heal. The Well has now been freed and cleared, the war for Earth's self-determination is over and won, and it's time to bring the Waters of Life back to us.

The Fire of Life at the Center of the Earth is our newest planetary grid. Its keeper is Lady Portia, also known as the

Goddess Hestia or Vesta, known in Greece and Rome as keeper of the hearth. The Fire of Life is the other aspect of the life force, along with the Well of Life, and the Fire is located in the core of the planet beneath the Well. Fire and water are not known to join or mix, but the Fire of Life rises through and joins with the Water of Life to become one stream. The White Fire is for purification of the life force, of the Earth and all people, while the waters of the Well are for healing and clearing away those energies no longer beneficial to our growth.

The Fire of Life and the Water of Life are part of our birthright as Be-ings on the Ascension path. The Water is creation and the Fire is transformation. Lady Portia is now keeper of the transformation of the planet, a job formerly done by Ascended Master St. Germaine. St. Germaine has taken over another of the planetary grids, the Transmutation Grid instead. He still is keeper of the Violet Flame, where Lady Portia's flame is white. The Water and Fire together are the cleansing and purification, the transformation, of our life force and the freeing of our creation and planetary destiny. The entities that have attacked and interfered with Earth since creation, the Source of All Evil, are now gone. We can take up our clearing, evolution, and Ascension as we were meant to do.

With this information in mind, it is time to go to the Lords of Karma and Divine Director to return the life force of the Well of Life and the Fire of Life to our energy and Be-ing. This has already been done for the planet and requested for all life. In the concept of critical mass, however, it is best for many individuals to ask for it themselves. This is a gentle and life-affirming process and request, despite the power and force these planetary grid structures suggest. Of course, you will not receive the full force of the elements, of Fire or Water, in your energy. No one could withstand that much power. Instead of the volcano you will be given the equivalent of a sunny day, and instead of the hurricane, spring rain.

Go to your meditation space, calm your mind and body, and establish your grounding cord. Visualize a cord running from your genitals between your legs into the Earth. Request the Lords of Karma and Divine Director that your grounding cord be fully extended and connected to the Center of the Earth and beyond. Use this wording, and make it a full Lords of Karma process. This is important. Your grounding cord is the central channel of your grounding system, your connection to Earth and Earth incarnation. It begins at your heart and runs downward through your body to below the Center of the Earth, if you are properly grounded and connected.

Being properly grounded means to be calm, open, and centered. It means having a quiet, receptive mind, a stable body, and the ability to hear psychically. It gives you the anchoring necessary to do psychic work safely, without risk of damage to your energy bodies and systems. The grounding cord is your first line of energy protection— when you are fully rooted, your life line is secure. Many people avoid being grounded, thinking that they can be more psychic when they are less connected to the Earth. Not only does this interfere with their ability to manage daily life, it reduces their psychic abilities and their psychic and physical safety, as well. When you are fully grounded, you have an anchor so that you can go further in your psychic explorations. It also gives you earthplane stability.

Some women—and it is primarily women—who have suffered incest, battering, or abuse find the idea of being grounded frightening. They would rather be free of their bodies, or at least free to leave them at a moment's notice. In times of abuse when things became intolerable, they removed their consciousness from what was happening to them and separated their souls from their bodies. It was the only defense and only escape possible. As adults, though the situations have ended, they are suspicious of anything that might prevent them from leaving if they need to. Men, on the other hand, tend to be too grounded. They need the ability and initiative to explore beyond the mundane; they need to know that they are more than physical, that they also have souls. Connecting the grounding cord to the Center of the Earth frees both those who wish to escape and those who are too grounded. It offers stability on Earth and the ability to take your consciousness to other levels of awareness.

The grounding cord is the physical part of your Galactic Cord system, and is joined to your Galactic Cord at the heart, as well. The Galactic Cord begins in the Heart Complex and extends upward through all your core soul levels. This cord is all of your connections with the Light, with the Goddess, Great Goddess, Great Mother, and All-Mother, the Ascended Masters, Lords of Karma and Divine Director, the angels and archangels, and the Radiance of the Light Beyond the Goddess. It extends to and beyond your creation, and through the Pure Light beyond Creation.

The grounding cord and Galactic Cord are the most vital components of your energy. Now ask the Lords of Karma and Divine Director to fully establish your Galactic Cord and all its components, to fully insulate them, and to establish and open all your optimal connections with the Light. Take this request through the full Lords of Karma process. If your psychic abilities are visual, you may see a shaft of light coming from above your head, moving into and through your body, and exiting your body to continue far below you. You may see it enter the planetary core. While we are all supposed to be connected in this way, few of us are and it is time now to establish, clear, and re-establish all these proper connections. Your psychic abilities, level of energy clearing and protection, and contact with all sources of the Light and all Light Be-ings will greatly increase from this time forth by making the two requests above.

Now ask the Lords of Karma and Divine Director to extend your grounding cord to and through the Well of Life and the Fire of Life at the Center of the Earth. You may feel or be shown visuals of this happening. Do the full Lords of Karma process with this request, and all requests, and don't forget to thank them. When this is complete, ask the Lords of Karma and Divine Director to bring what you can optimally handle of the life force, the Water and the Fire, into and through your energy in a continuous and permanent way. Remember to seal the request unto the Light and unto protection forever. Stay in the meditative state while these energy flows are established. Then, it's best to go to bed and let the healing and energy clearing continue through the night. You may be kept awake while the process goes on, but you will not be tired or exhausted from it tomorrow. You have been granted a great gift and a major step in your energy evolution, as well as in the evolution, clearing, and protection of the planet.

The next process is from *Essential Energy Balancing*. While a version of it is used in *Essential Energy Balancing* as the second process, this version is more advanced and detailed, and is taken from the forthcoming *Healing the Goddess*. Its intent is to bring clearing and Light through every component and aspect of your energy system. The names of many of these components will be new to you. Rather than spend a great deal of time on explanations, I can only suggest that you read *Essential Energy Balancing* and study the many charts and diagrams on energy structure given in the last part of the book. As you go through the clearing process you will feel or be shown what is happening and what the components mean.

Our energy is composed of many layers and bodies. Each layer has its own series of chakras, and many connections and channels. The templates connect these layers and levels, and all the layers and bodies are eventually interconnected. The layers that comprise an onion are the best analogy I can offer of how this looks and works. The Tube of Light is the whole energy structure of the core soul; the Crystal Shaft is the outer surface of that tube and the rest of the components are inside it. I have already described the Galactic Cord and grounding systems. Where the clearing methods of the last chapter are primarily for your closer-to-physical levels of energy, the Essential Energy Balancing process given below is designed for total energy clearing, up to and including the soul levels.

This clearing sequence should be done at night in meditation before bedtime. Every night is not too often to do it, and I recommend doing it at least once a week. It takes about half an hour to complete, though sometimes it can take longer if there is a lot being cleared from your energy. It is a Lords of Karma and Divine Director process but with a difference. Here are simple directions to be read exactly as given below, without the usual finishing steps of a karmic request. You will read the steps and they will be accomplished as you ask for them. Unless you get a no, you will probably not receive a response, but what you ask for will happen immediately.

If you receive a no, it is probably because you are moving too fast through the process. You must complete each step before going to the next one. You will know when you are ready to move forward by sensations of energy reaching your feet. The clearing for each step starts in your head and moves down. If you do not wait for the energy to reach your feet before making the next request, you will not be permitted to proceed. With any other no response, ask the Lords of Karma and Divine Director what to do and follow their instructions. You will be pleased at how you feel when this meditation is finished. Do it often.

If at any step it feels as if the energy is stopped or not moving, ask what may be wrong. Is there blockage or obstruction there? Is something disconnected, damaged, or in need of healing, repair, or replacement? Do you simply need to wait longer for the clearing to be finished? Ask these questions of the Lords of Karma, using a pendulum if you need to. If you discover something wrong, ask them to fix the problem at the source. Wait for them to do it, or ask them whether you should go on or wait. Ask them if you are to continue the clearing—sometimes the purpose of the clearing is to find what is wrong and to heal it. If you are not to continue, ask if you should do an energy clearing the next night. Use this process as an all-energy diagnostic system as well as for all-energy clearing. Now begin the process, using the precise wording given below.

TOTAL ENERGY CLEARING

• Ask the Lords of Karma and Divine Director to clear, heal, align, open, activate, synchronize, fill with Light, repair, and reconnect your entire Tube of Light and Crystal Shaft, and all the chakras, chakra complexes, channels, connections, and templates through all levels and all systems. (Wait until the energy reaches your feet before going on.)

• Ask the Lords of Karma and Divine Director to clear, heal, align, open, activate, synchronize, fill with Light, repair, and reconnect your grounding cord on all levels to the Center of the Earth and beyond, including all planetary structures, grid structures, and connections, and all the chakras, chakra complexes, channels, connections, and templates through all levels and all systems. (Wait until the energy reaches your feet before going on. Wait after each step.)

• Ask the Lords of Karma and Divine Director to clear, heal, align, open, activate, synchronize, fill with Light, repair, and reconnect your templates on all levels, and all the chakras, chakra complexes, channels, and connections through all levels and all systems. List the following templates one by one, going to the next only after the previous template is cleared. Keep them in strict order.

> Ka template
> Etheric template
> Ketheric template
> Celestial template
> I-Am template
> All Galactic chakras and templates on all levels
> All Causal Body chakras and templates on all levels
> All Ascension chakras and templates on all levels

• Ask the Lords of Karma and Divine Director to clear, heal, align, open, activate, synchronize, fill with Light, repair, and reconnect your: Silver Cord and chakras down the back on all levels, and all the chakras, chakra complexes, channels, connections, and templates through all levels and all systems.

• Ask the Lords of Karma and Divine Director to clear, heal, align, open, activate, synchronize, fill with Light, repair, and reconnect your: heart complex, heart panels, and all heart systems on all levels, and all the chakras, chakra complexes, channels, connections, and templates through all levels and all systems.

• Ask the Lords of Karma and Divine Director to clear, heal, align, open, activate, synchronize, fill with Light, repair, and reconnect your: Physical and Etheric bodies, and all the chakras, chakra complexes, channels, connections, and templates through all levels and all systems. List the following chakras one by one, going on only after the previous chakra is fully cleared and you feel the energy reach your feet:

Crown Chakra, chakra complex, and chakra system through all levels and all systems

Third Eye Chakra, chakra complex, and chakra system through all levels and all systems

Throat Chakra, chakra complex, and chakra system through all levels and all systems

Heart Chakra, chakra complex, and chakra system through all levels and all systems

Solar Plexus Chakra, chakra complex, and chakra system through all levels and all systems

Belly Chakra, chakra complex, and chakra system through all levels and all systems

Root Chakra, chakra complex, and chakra system through all levels and all systems, to the Center of the Earth and beyond

• Ask the Lords of Karma and Divine Director to clear, heal, align, open, activate, synchronize, fill with Light, repair, and reconnect your: Emotional and Astral bodies, and all the chakras, chakra complexes, channels, connections, and templates through all levels and all systems. List the following chakras one by one, going to the next only after the previous chakra is cleared. Be sure to keep them in order.

Transpersonal Point Chakra, chakra complex, and chakra system through all levels and all systems

Vision Chakras (2), chakra complex, and chakra system through all levels and all systems

Causal Body Chakra, chakra complex, and chakra system through all levels and all systems

Thymus Chakra, chakra complex, and chakra system through all levels and all systems

Diaphragm Chakra, chakra complex, and chakra system through all levels and all systems

Hara Chakra, chakra complex, and chakra system through all levels and all systems

Perineum Chakra, chakra complex, and chakra system through all levels and all systems

Movement Chakras (2), chakra complex, and chakra system through all levels and all systems

Grounding Chakras (2), chakra complex, and chakra system through all levels and all systems, to the Center of the Earth and beyond

Earth Chakras (2), chakra complex, and chakra system through all levels and all systems, to the Center of the Earth and beyond

• Ask the Lords of Karma and Divine Director to clear, heal, align, open, activate, synchronize, fill with Light, repair, and reconnect your: Mental Body and Mind Grid, and all the chakras, chakra complexes, channels, connections, and templates through all levels and all systems. List the following chakras one by one, going to the next only after the previous chakra is cleared. These chakras are not Kundalini (Etheric Body) chakras, but their Mental Body and Mind Grid counterparts.

Crown Chakra, Crown complex, and Crown system through all levels and all systems

Third Eye Chakra, Third Eye complex, and Third Eye system through all levels and all systems

Light Chakras (2), Light complex, and Light system through all levels and all systems

Chakras at the top of the Throat, the lips, and lower Throat and entire Throat complex, and Throat system through all levels and all systems

Solar Plexus Chakra, Solar Plexus complex, and Solar Plexus system through all levels and all systems. (Note: There is no heart or heart equivalent on the Mental Body or Mind Grid levels.)

Root Chakra, Root complex, and all Root systems through all levels and all systems, to the Center of the Earth and beyond

All chakras, chakra complexes, and chakra systems through all levels and all systems for the breasts, fingers, and toes

• Ask the Lords of Karma and Divine Director to clear, heal, align, open, activate, synchronize, fill with Light, repair, and reconnect your: Spiritual, Galactic, and Causal Bodies, and all the chakras, chakra complexes, channels, connections, and templates through all levels and all systems. The chakras for these are as follows, in sets rather than individually:

All the chakras, chakra complexes, and chakra systems on all levels and through all systems for the chakras of Will, Desire, Attainment, Action, and Propulsion, to the Center of the Earth and beyond. (These are the Galactic Body chakras.)

All the chakras, chakra complexes, and chakra systems through all levels and all systems for the chakras of Sound, Reception/information, Communication, Manifestation, Creation, and Implementation. (These are the Causal Body chakras.)

The Spiritual, Galactic, and Causal Body Crown Chakra, Crown complex, and Crown system through all levels and all systems.

• Ask the Lords of Karma and Divine Director to clear, heal, align, open, activate, synchronize, fill with Light, repair, and reconnect your: Ascension on all levels, and all the chakras, chakra complexes, channels, connections, templates, and components of all Ascension processes through all levels and all systems. (Note: The Ascension processes operate through all the bodies. To request clearing for only the Ascension Body would be to limit this request for clearing.) When the Ascension levels are fully cleared, the energy clearing is complete. To finish, make one last request.

• Ask the Lords of Karma and Divine Director to fill your energy with the Radiance of the Light Beyond the Goddess through all the levels and components of your Be-ing, through all dimensions, all connections, and all systems.

• Thank the Lords of Karma and Divine Director, and end your meditation. This process is best done when you are lying down at night, just before you got to sleep. You may do it in bed if you wish to.

This is the most complete energy clearing process you can do, and though it takes a bit of time, it is well worth the effort. It will leave you with a sense of positive well-being for several days. The more often you can do this process—nightly is not too often—the better. It is a form of the more familiar practice of "running energy" but far more thorough. It will also teach you a great deal about your own energy anatomy. As you do each step you will feel the energy moving through you and begin to understand how complex and marvelous your nonphysical anatomy is. The requests to clear, heal, align, open, activate, synchronize, fill with Light, repair, and reconnect go a long way toward healing all aura rips and tears and all energy damage through the bodies. All the energy components are included in the requests through more levels than most energy clearing systems reach. The process does more than simply clearing your energy—it is a method of healing all the components of your energy system through both closer-to-physical and outer core soul levels.

There is a further request you may make to protect your chakras. Ask the Lords of Karma and Divine Director to place a filter of Light on each of your Kundalini chakras. Specify that this filter is to prevent the entrance of all negative and harmful energies, while clearing and removing from each chakra all negative and harmful energies already present on all levels and through all systems. Again, use the wording I have given. Take the request through the full Lords of Karma and Divine Director process. As with the home protection dome, which this shielding is a variant of, you want to make sure that only negative energy is blocked, allowing the Light to come in. You also want to allow for a way in which any negative energies already in the chakras can be removed, and all the chakras cleared.

Use this only for the Kundalini chakras. If you wish to name them, the seven Kundalini chakras are: the Crown (top of the head), Third Eye (forehead above and between the eyes), Throat (center of the throat), Heart (between the breasts), Solar Plexus (below the breasts, center of the body), Belly chakra (below the navel, center of the body), and Root chakra (the genitals).

You may extend this shielding to protect each energy body with the following request. Ask the Lords of Karma and Divine Director to place a filter of Light around each of your energy bodies. Specify that this filter is to prevent the entrance of all negative and harmful energies, while clearing and removing from each body all negative and harmful energies already present on all levels and through all systems. Use the above wording, and take the request through the full Lords of Karma and Divine Director process. With both of these processes, request that all clearing be gentle and easy, and happen in the best possible way. This is to prevent a clearing that may be too rapid for comfort.

There are fifty-five energy bodies, but the ones relevant to this request (in pairs) are the Physical and Etheric Bodies, the Emotional and Astral Bodies, the Mental Body and Mind Grid, the Spiritual, Galactic, and Causal Bodies, and the Ascension Body. For a more thorough discussion of the energy bodies and the chakra systems on each of them, see *Essential Energy Balancing*.

As often as you can remember to do it, ask the Lords of Karma and Divine Director to fill your energy, through all levels, components, and systems with so much Light that no negativity can enter, remain, or exist there. Ask frequently to be filled with the healing of the Water of Life and the White Fire purification of the Fire of Life at the Center of the Earth. A cleared, healed aura that is filled with Light is protected from most negative interference and evil. As the full reconnection of your DNA continues, more clearing and healing takes place and your Light vibrational level increases. By the time that you have cleared, healed, reconnected, and activated twenty-four strands of your DNA, you will be fully protected from the negative dark.

7

KARMIC CLEARING

Almost everything that happens to us can be explained by karma. Each person we meet and interact with, each life situation we are presented with, our character traits and habits, and all dis-eases and physical conditions are karmic. We are given free will and intelligence, and expected to use these things to free ourselves and to resolve the things that hold us back. But often free will takes many lifetimes, and when patterns and relationships become entrenched, neither free will nor intelligence is enough. Negative interference and its effects upon our lives and upon our energy systems is also karmic. Rather than trying to push the river, let's work with the karmic sources and end the negativity at its roots.

Most negative interference of human origin derives from relationships. Relationships are the center of our lives and our many lifetimes, and they repeat through lifetime after lifetime. Our lifetimes interconnect and so do our interactions with people, the same people appearing again and again through our incarnational herstories. Where a good and loving relationship can be the joy of a lifetime, and the return of a love is the joy of many incarnations, relationships gone wrong can also be the bane that follows us from incarnation to incarnation. Just as someone we loved in the past may appear in multiple lifetimes, so can someone we hated or who hated us, or who hurt us terribly.

Most karma revolves around hurt and damage that was not healed in the lifetime where it began. Because it was not healed it appears again, presenting the opportunity both for more hurt and to heal and resolve it so it ends. Hurt and damage usually means karma with other people, mostly people who have hurt us before and will continue to do so until we end our karma with them. Karma that requires people to do to or with each other what they have done before, for the purpose of bringing a situation to resolution, is called a karmic contract.

Our Akashic Records, the records of our soul's many incarnations on Earth and other planets, is a collection of karmic contracts. A selection of these contracts is presented for resolution in each incarnation, with hope that enough of them will be cleared to ease and end a great deal of suffering. Once the resolution is met, the negative situation does not have to be repeated. The same person does not have to reincarnate with you again to repeat whatever went wrong in the relationship. These situations are generally not victim and villain deals. It can take two to tango. We have all done wrong things, we have all misjudged others, we have all been in conflict with someone, we have all felt we were right. When two people with opposite views feel they are right and insist on having their own way, karma usually follows.

No one is expected to be perfect. We are only expected to be human. Very few people are evil, and none of us is created evil. The things we do wrong are only a part of how we learn, a part of the process of being human. We are expected to do the best we can, and most people do just that. That we mess up is only part of the game, it does not make us "evil sinners," or in any way unloved by the Light and the Goddess. It just is. And when

we are part of a situation, we simply have to learn to get ourselves out of it. Getting ourselves out of it has in the past taken
a very long time, lifetimes and sometimes many lifetimes. In this
life, however, we have the opportunity to finish a lot of karma
very quickly.

The key to doing this, of course, is the dispensation for just
about everything now being granted to us by the Lords of
Karma. This is an incredibly great gift. All we need to do to be
released from some very difficult things is to ask for it. First,
however, we need to realize what is wrong in our lives. When we
look at each of our current relationships, we get a pretty good
view of what is wrong, as well as what is right. By tracing back
to the source of our not-so-good relationships, by finding the
karmic contracts that caused things to go wrong, we are given
both realization and release. And it's a very important release
indeed.

In order to attain Ascension, the ending of the requirement
to reincarnate, we must clear, heal, and be released from more
than 50 percent of our Earth karma. In the process of recon-
necting the first sections of our DNA, the first twelve strands,
those karmas still to be cleared are presented to us for healing.
The situations come forward, or the awareness that something
is wrong and that we need help with it. We are expected to work
cooperatively with the Lords of Karma to acknowledge where
things are wrong in our lives, and to work closely with them to
heal it. When we do our part in this, we will be led to the information we need for the clearing.

When the second section of DNA is reconnected and activated, twenty-one strands, our karmic contracts from other
planets are also activated. A whole new set of situations comes
forward for healing. Anything that has not been cleared in six
months by working diligently with the Lords of Karma is no

longer Earth karma. It is karma from other-planet lifetimes. Anything that you are granted by the Lords of Karma that does not change in a reasonable time period is likely karma not from Earth. This is where Divine Director comes in, as the arbitrator of other-planet karma. While we will have less awareness of other-planet incarnations and situations, the karma left from these lifetimes is usually the source of some very deep suffering on Earth. It also usually involves karma with people that may be very disturbing, that involves a great deal of negative interference and even evil.

Nevertheless, with Divine Director we are given the opportunity for some very rapid healing and clearing of karma that has held us back for many lifetimes. The same people who have presented problems in our Earth incarnations may appear in other-planetary ones. The same evils that harmed us from other-planet sources may replicate from the far distant past into our present Earth life. They are doing so now because we have the means to clear these karmas and end their damage, evil, and harm forever. Anytime a negative past life situation comes up, from Earth or any other planet, consider it pain leaving. Go to the Lords of Karma and Divine Director to clear it at the source, and be very grateful when it's done.

The key to healing long-term karmic patterns from Earth or that have followed us to Earth is canceling our karmic contracts with the source. Here is the precise phrasing to use in these requests: ask to "cancel all karma and all karmic contracts, from Earth and all other planets, from all lifetimes and between them with the source of the difficulty or damage." By asking to do this, you will instantly end karmic patterns and suffering from many lifetimes that have severely affected your current life. You will end it forever. If the karmic contract is with a person, or with negative interference from a person, you will instantly end their ability to harm you, the damage they have caused, and all of your contact with that person forever.

You will obviously not cancel your karmic contracts with someone you love and wish to continue interacting with. You may however, ask to cancel all of your *negative* karma and karmic contracts with that person. For most difficult relationships, this is usually very successful and all that is needed. If you ask to cancel all karma and all karmic contracts, that person will be totally and irrevocably removed from your karma and your life. This is serious stuff. Be careful how you use it. Sometimes, however, that canceling of all contracts forever with a source of great harm can cause and promote the deepest healing you have ever experienced. The situations that come forward for these healings will be only the tough stuff, requiring tough solutions for your healing, release, and freedom.

To give you an example, my father abused me severely through my early life and though I eventually removed myself from his presence totally the damage still remained. As I learned to work with the Lords of Karma, I asked repeatedly to heal my karma and all the damage from my father and it was granted, but much of the physical and emotional damage continued. I asked for karmic severance with him and it was granted, but nothing in the damage changed. Though I asked repeatedly about past lives with him, I was told there were none. From my experience with karma this seemed impossible but I was shown no other lifetimes. I assumed there was something I wasn't ready to see and that it would come up later.

When I began working with Divine Director, I asked again to clear my karma with all the people who were seriously harmful in my Earth lifetimes. I asked this time to cancel all karma and all karmic contracts with my father, from Earth and all other planets. This time I hit pay dirt. I saw a lifetime where as a very small child my father hung me until I died. (I was battered unconscious in this lifetime as a small child and left with neurological and vision damage.) I asked for karmic release from that lifetime and from the abuser. Next, I was shown my father, in that off-planet life or some other, being consumed through his anger and rage into a nonhuman entity, something with glowing red eyes. There was no human soul. That entity followed me through a number of reincarnations, doing similar damage each time. He was male and adult and I was female and a child in each lifetime, and there were several more brutal murders.

The evil in the entity followed me through many incarnations and planets to harm other people, harming so many that it created a force for great evil on the Earth. The entity grew stronger and stronger, and I named it the Negative Form. Part of my job, my karmic contract, for this incarnation was to end the replication of it on this planet. In his current Earth lifetime my father carried a small part of that seed, and many other people also carried it. I asked to cancel all karma and all karmic contracts with this Negative Form, and with those other people I found it in. All of those people have attacked and harmed me. Eventually through Divine Director, I was able to remove the entity from Earth and from all Earth people. I was able to clear it from my current father, as well. The damage will heal now in all of us. When I asked for the reason for all this, I was told that sometimes Light has to come from the negative darkness—and to heal it.

When you are shown situations of karma from other planets, you will find that people are still people, not noticeably different from what humans are like on Earth. I found that I was shown situations that could have happened on Earth or anywhere else, at almost any historical time. If I hadn't been told that these were other-planet lifetimes I would not have known it. These were still human situations. (The nonhuman, negative entities are just as bizarre from Earth as they are from other places.) I found, however, that the situations from other planets that remain to affect our current lives are extremely intensive situations. These aren't just a matter of dealing with someone you didn't get along with in the past in another place—these are real blockbusters.

I also found that once these off-planet sources of severe situations were found and the release of them was granted, major positive changes in my life happened quickly. Beforehand, I felt all progress in my life and healing had stopped. It suddenly took off again—at high speed. I have been severely energy attacked and psychic attacked in this lifetime and found the source of all these attacks originated on other planets. Though the attacks on Earth seemed to come from several people, they all had a central source that was not of Earth. Nothing I could do in working with Earth karma ended the attacks, but working with Divine Director did it, and did it not only for myself but for the planet, as well. Rather than being afraid when these lifetimes and the connections between them surfaced, I became fascinated by the pieces of a puzzle coming together for completion. I will not be attacked, damaged, murdered, or abused again.

Since you have included both the Lords of Karma and Divine Director in all of your requests in this book, you have probably cleared a great deal of karma from other planets already. If you have been working diligently, asking to heal all the things that are wrong in your life, much has already changed. From this point on, of anything that remains to be healed, start inquiring if the karma you are clearing is from Earth or not from Earth. If it has not healed with the process given in Chapter 2, ask if you need to take the situation further. Do you need to use the karma clearing process for lifetimes off-planet? Is a simple request directly to Divine Director enough?

If you need to go further, the process follows. It is a shortened and condensed version of what was originally given to me in many steps, with a great many more words.

OTHER-PLANET KARMA

First, ask to speak with the Lords of Karma and Divine Director, as you usually do in any karmic release. When you perceive their presence, use the following formula to make your request:

I ask to cancel all karma and all karmic contracts at the source with (the person or situation) from Earth and all other planets and between them, all lifetimes and between them, through all multidimensions and between them of my multidimensional Be-ing.

I ask for the healing to be
Fully, completely, permanently, and forever,
Through all the levels and components of my Be-ing,
All dimensions, all connections, all systems,
And between them, through all lifetimes and between
them, through all multidimensions and between them of my
multidimensional Be-ing.

I ask for the healing
Immediately and instantly,
Past present and future,
NOW.

Wait for your response at the end. Be sure to say thank you. If you are told no, ask for further instructions. Never force it if you receive a no response. The wording must be kept in exactly this way, including the repetitions. For most people there will be very few things left to clear with this process if you have been working at clearing your karma this far. The things that do clear with it, however, will be profound. You may or may not be shown other planets and situations, but if you are granted the request, it is done.

When you ask to cancel a karmic contract that is not from Earth, and the request is granted, you will experience something you may not have known before. (If you have gone through the Essential Energy Balancing processes, this will not be new to you.) As soon as your request is granted, your Crown chakra will be closed for four hours for rewiring and repatterning. This is uncomfortable, as you will lose your psychic abilities for the time. When you do your release work the last thing at night, this closing up can be done overnight and you may never be aware of it. If you ask for a number of clearings (I recommend this so that you finish it all at once, as fast as possible), the closing up may last longer. It is nothing to fear and there is nothing you can do about it. Just wait for it to end and go about your day. It will not interfere with your earthplane life in any way, only your psychic life. During this time, you will not be able to do energy clearing, but you may make other karma requests.

There are three ways to clear psychic attacks: to repair your aura and fill it with Light, to clear and protect your home and environment, and to break all ties and holds upon you by your attacker. We have done the first two of these in other chapters, and the canceling of karmic contracts—from Earth and all other planets—completes the third. Now that you have ended your karma with devastating situations and people from this and other lifetimes, it is time to clear your energy and break their last hold upon you.

To do so is to remove all negative cords and hooks from your chakras. This is not a new process, but we will take it further than is usual here and look at it in a new way. Cords are connections by other people to your energy, connections made through the chakras. These exist primarily on the Kundalini line of your Etheric Double, the closest energy level to your physical body. Psychically, these look like strings or telephone wires coming from your energy, and you will find another person at the end of each of them. Some of these people will surprise you. They can be people you have a lot of interaction with or people you may have met once at the supermarket. They all want something from you, however, consciously or not, and it should be up to you to decide if you want to give it to them. There will be positive cords, to people you love and are lovingly involved with, but here we will ask only to see and remove the negative ones.

People attach these cords to you for various reasons. Someone who wants something from you will "cord" you. They may want you to give them road directions somewhere, or they may want to drain energy from you. They may be totally innocent, or not. At the end of every day, with our interactions with many people, we may have a multitude of cords. These cords are simple to flick off, just ask the Lords of Karma to clear you of them and do it frequently. You may ask the Lords of Karma to remove all negative cords from you and keep you clear of them forever. At this level, they are Earth karma only.

When you reach the next energy level, the Emotional/Astral level, instead of cords you may find hooks in your chakras. These are much more serious, and each hook represents someone whom you have incarnated with for some seriously negative reason. Though none of these hooks will be positive, we will still ask to clear only negative ones. Each hook represents a karmic contract, still from Earth at this level. When you find a hook in your Hara Chakra, it is to a person who seeks to keep you from fulfilling your life path. You may be surprised at who some of these people are. You will have much fewer hooks than cords at the lower level, but they will represent significant karma and damage to your life. To remove these will free you in many ways.

The next energy system is the Mental Body and Mind Grid level, and there may be hooks (no cords) on this level as well. Again, they will be fewer than on the level below them. These hooks begin to represent karmic contracts with people from other-planet lifetimes. As with the Kundalini and Emotional/Astral hooks, you will know who these people are. As you may realize, the higher into your core soul energy you go with these things, the more serious the karma and the situation.

You may also find hooks in your Spiritual, Galactic, or Causal Body chakras. These are the spiritual body levels and very far away from the physical body. These involve highly negative karma from other-planet incarnations, and you may or may not know the people connected to them. You may not even be shown who they are. As with all chakra cords and hooks, these are karmic contracts with people, rather than with situations or lifetimes. At this level, they restrict and do harm to your spiritual path; they are the source of serious long-term psychic attack and clearing them is a major healing.

In your meditation space, ask to speak with the Lords of Karma and Divine Director. Make the following request: Ask the Lords of Karma and Divine Director to "Gently dissolve and remove from your chakras and energy on all levels and through all systems, all negative cords and hooks from Earth and all other planets, through all lifetimes and between them." Ask for "the healing to be through all multidimensions and between them of your multidimensional Be-ing." Ask for it "fully, completely, permanently, and forever, through all the levels and components of your Be-ing, all dimensions, all connections, all systems and between them, through all lifetimes and between them, of and between all dimensions of your multidimensional Be-ing." Ask for "the healing immediately and instantly, past present and future, NOW." (The repetitions in the wording are needed.) Specify that "the healing be done very gently and without discomfort, in the best possible now."

In a further process, ask to "Cancel all *negative* karma and karmic contracts with all sources of these cords and hooks." Specify negative. If you are shown a situation and wish to do more, ask Divine Director "if it is appropriate to ask to cancel *all* karma and all karmic contracts," and only do so if he agrees. Remember that to do this means to end your connection with that person forever. In many or even most cases this is desirable, but make sure before you do it.

As these cords and hooks clear, you may be shown what people they came from. Sometimes the cords or hooks will not be released until you are made aware of who they are and given the chance to understand what happened. You will also be able to keep any cords or hooks that you wish to. Remember, however, that we have asked to release only the negative ones, and if you are shown that something is negative, it's a good idea to let it go. Occasionally this can be difficult, as sometimes the hook is from someone important in your present life, a parent or a mate, or someone you truly love. Remember that at this point you are only releasing the hooks, not the people themselves. If you then ask to cancel all karma and all karmic contracts with the person, you are releasing the person from your karma and your life, too. You will make these choices freely but you may be pushed into some of these for your own good and growth.

The clearing moves from level to level. First you will be shown the cords on the Kundalini line/Etheric Double chakras. These are the most minor. They will be people you work with, minor friends, acquaintances. Some may be people you never remember meeting. If someone is draining energy from you and you remove the cord, that person may get very angry. They have lost the free ride at your expense. Your previous shielding will keep you from harm, or you can simply insist (psychically or otherwise) that the person leave.

As you move into each higher level the hooks become increasingly deeper and with more serious consequences. You may discover that your inability to make a living has something to do with someone's hook in your energy, or your chronic fatigue, or your continued pattern of being abused, or your difficulties in finding a mate. These are serious things, and it will create much positive change to end them. You may be shown why these people are in your life and what effect they have had. You may be shown the source of the relationship. If you don't need to know, you may only be shown the hooks and watch them being removed. If you need to understand, or to know who put the hook there or why, you will be shown. If you are not shown anything, but the request was granted, trust that it is being done. You will most likely feel the work happening in your energy.

Make very sure that when you ask for cords and hooks to be removed, you ask that it be done gently. It is possible that the clearing will not be done all at once but over a three-day period or longer. Before I knew the Lords of Karma or Divine Director, I asked to remove a hook that I saw on my Hara Line (Emotional Body level). At that time, I didn't know what hooks were, only that they shouldn't be there, and that the object in question was causing me harm. I knew that the hook in my Hara chakra was from my mother and that it was there to impede my writing. So I insisted it be taken out immediately. I psychically watched it go, then spent the next three days sick and nauseous, feeling as if I had been ripped in half a few times. When I saw more hooks later, I didn't know how to proceed. When you ask the Lords of Karma and Divine Director to do this in a gentle way, they will dissolve the hooks instead of ripping them out. You will not get sick.

I did not know at that time that negative cords and hooks represent karmic contracts with people, and that some of those contracts did not originate on Earth. Now that you know this, you will have information about your life you never had before. You will have some understanding as to why things have happened as they have, and why they have not changed no matter how hard you have worked to change them. You will also have a way to change them. As I said earlier, I am no longer being psychically attacked, primarily because of the working with Divine Director to clear other-planet karma and karmic contracts with some very negative people who have followed me through multiple lifetimes.

You may wish to check your energy from time to time and repeat the request to clear all negative cords and hooks. Cords can return, but will be usually only minor, but hooks do not come back. However, it can also happen that you've missed something the first time. Maybe you weren't ready to clear the contracts with a particular person, or maybe a series of other things had to be cleared first. It's wise to check again occasionally to see that all cords and hooks through all levels and all systems are truly gone.

You may also ask the Lords of Karma and Divine Director that no more cords or hooks ever be placed in your chakras on any level from Earth or any other planet or lifetime or between them again. This is a good request to make. Take it through the standard Lords of Karma and Divine Director process, and then follow it with the off-planet karmic contract process. The two processes do different things, and doing both is good insurance. (If you need to do this with other requests, you will know.) You may also ask to extend your chakra shields to prevent the reattachment of old or attachment of new chakra cords. Your shields are only on the Kundalini chakras, but new hooks on other levels begin as Kundalini cords. To prevent them from forming at all is an important healing.

It is important to understand how and why cords attach to you and how they become hooks. Cords are from this life on Earth. They are from people who want something from you. If they are minor acquaintances, they are inconsequential and will wither and fade simply with any Light or energy work you may do. If they are from people you have a relationship with, they may be more tenacious. If the relationship becomes important, and the person cording you insists on holding on, insists on what they want, the cords can dig deeper into your energy. If that cord comes from someone who proves to be a difficult or particularly negative relationship, and if that relationship is not resolved in this life, the cord can become a hook in the next life.

In the beginning, that cord or hook is easy to release, but if it is not released and the relationship is reinforced by other negative interactions through other lifetimes without resolution, the cord becomes a hook and the hook moves higher and higher into your energy system. The longer it is there, the more bad lifetimes with the person, the deeper the hook, the higher it goes into your energy, and the harder it is to remove. Cords on the Kundalini line are the easiest to clear, but hooks in the Spiritual Body chakras may be very difficult. Hooks from that high in your energy, too, have followed you through lifetimes on other planets.

In my understanding, we must complete almost all of our karma incurred on a planet before we are freed from reincarnation there. If a hook is present in your energy from one or more lifetimes on other planets, it is a very significant karma indeed.

These are the people who have held back your evolution for lifetimes, who have robbed you of your freedom and spiritual growth, who have attacked, murdered, and abused you repeatedly. You probably know them in this lifetime if they have followed you so far. Your life will take a great change for the better with the canceling of these karmic contracts and the removal of the karmic hooks. This is a major energy protection indeed.

You now have achieved the three ways to clear yourself of psychic attack. You have repaired your aura, protected and cleared your home, and broken the hold of most of your attackers from your energy. Still there is more to do, but if you go no further, you have come a long way into the Light. The next chapter discusses clearing yourself of deliberate negative interference.

8

DELIBERATE INTERFERENCE

Someone who hates you can disrupt your life. This is true on an earthplane level and even more true on a psychic level. On a psychic level the disruption can continue over lifetimes; on a karmic level that person and their hatred can follow you around the Universe for centuries. These are not unconsidered statements. If you have done the work of the last chapter you have seen the hooks in your chakras and been surprised and probably shocked at whom they came from and what they did to you. The worst are those people who have obstructed your life purpose, your service to others or the planet. We live for a dual purpose, to learn and evolve ethically and spiritually, and to help others and the planet to do so, as well. Our greatest lesson is to love, and sometimes our greatest lessons in loving are about being hated.

It is unethical to return someone's hate; you must protect and heal yourself from it in other ways. To return hate for hate only entangles you with more of the same, and it makes you as wrong as the person hating you. In Wicca we have a law, which is also Karmic Law: "What you send out returns tenfold." Some say threefold, but the idea is the same. In Christianity the same law reads, "Do unto others as you would have them do unto you." Hate always returns. Negativity always returns. Don't let it return to you. Your job is to stay in the Light, to use the Light to clear and protect you. Establish your protection domes and shields. Clear your karma of all who offer you harm. Clear your karma of all hatreds of your own. Fill your energy with Light so the negative dark cannot reach you. But let the Lords of Karma and the Goddess take care of the offenders. They will always be taken care of, and in ways far more thorough than what you could devise or imagine.

I once witnessed a "hexing," the most chilling thing I have ever experienced. During a workshop, I was with a group of women at dinner and we were talking about a serial rapist who was then loose in one of the women's home towns. A friend of the woman telling the story had been raped and her community was working to heal her of the trauma. "We cannot allow this," the woman said, "we will stop it now." Our group was at a Chinese restaurant and the woman opened her fortune cookie. The cookie said something about women belonging on their backs; it was offensive at best. She said, "We will include this one, too, and all those who harm women."

She next took out a match and lit it. Over her dinner plate she held the fortune cookie tag in the tiny flame, and we watched it flare up. "You and all like you who harm women," she intoned, "I put you in the flame." This was not a joke and no one took it for one. A chill went through me. I condemn rapists or chauvinists and have always fought for women's protection and rights. Yet the hex to me was very wrong. I had a vision of this woman in a past life being burned to death as a witch. More flames. Many of us died that way, usually because we were independent, refused someone powerful who wanted us sexually, grew old and unwanted, had healing or psychic abilities, or someone was jealous. Most who died in the Inquisition weren't witches, just women. The woman lighting the match had died in that way, maybe at the hand of the man she was cursing, but somehow she

124

didn't learn the lesson. The rapist was finally caught, while I suppose the fortune cookie writer and others like him continue to belittle women. The incident stays in my mind twenty years later as a warning. What you send out comes back to you.

It is not Witches who set spells against others, who hex, make curses, do psychic attacks, use symbols to harm, or do evil in rituals. It is just the opposite, in fact. A Witch simply belongs to the pre-Christian religion that worships and honors the Goddess. Wicca is a religion that respects life and has an extremely strict awareness of karma and ethics. There are very few Wiccan laws, but they all speak of the right use of energy, and they are the basis of every other religion's ethics: "What you send out comes back to you," "Harming none, do what you will," or just simply "Harm none."

I have experienced curses, hexes, symbols used for attack and harm, negative rituals, distorting mind enchantments, and harmful spells. They are all varieties of psychic attack, are all negative interference and evil, and I have experienced far too many direct attacks, as well. Many people disbelieve the reality of these things, but I have learned otherwise. Focused energy can do great good in the world, it is the basis of psychic healing. Energy focused for harm can also do great harm. Magick is defined as the shaping of consciousness by will. Energy is thought and thought can be shaped consciously. It can be shaped for good or for wrong. Everything I teach and do is directed at using energy and consciousness ethically to protect and to heal. Not everyone has this awareness. This chapter is about understanding and protecting yourself from these evils.

My first awareness of having a curse placed upon me came from a group of born-again Christians. I did a lecture tour through Oregon, probably within a year of the Chinese restaurant hexing, almost twenty years ago. There were ten lectures in two weeks, each in a different small town or college. The lectures were for women, and three Christian women followed me from lecture to lecture, disrupting each one. They wanted to know why I wore eyeglasses since I said I could heal myself. They insisted on lists of books to read, proofs of the things I believed and spoke about; I was told later that they would take these books from libraries and destroy them. They told me repeatedly that they were praying for me, and by the end of the two weeks of lectures, they said they were praying to God for me to die so I could be saved. No one threw them out of the lectures, and I was too inexperienced at that time to do so myself. I tried not to show that their interference upset me, though it did, but I wasn't really frightened of them, either.

The morning after their first appearance at a lecture, I woke up with what I thought was the flu. I was nauseous, weak, and sick, and remained sick throughout the tour. By the time the first week was up I was having difficulties with my vision, and by the end of the two weeks I couldn't read. I thought I was just tired, or needed my eyeglasses changed. I went home and the nausea ended, but the fatigue from the trip never really seemed to go away. I developed a fear of public speaking, which I'd never had before, and though I continued teaching workshops, I stopped doing lectures. My vision continued to worsen, despite new glasses, into what became a hellish two years of not being able to focus my vision for reading at all. Several expensive months of vision therapy gave me back my reading ability at the end of that time. I never connected any of this with the Christian hecklers, and I forgot about them.

About five years after the Oregon trip, I received a psychic healing, and the woman doing the healing for me asked who had "put a hex" upon me. I didn't know what she was talking about. She said, "I see something in your Solar Plexus that looks like a black arrow with a string coming from it. The energy all around it looks like pus, green and festered. Who comes into your mind?" she asked. The good Christians did. "Follow the string," the healer suggested, "see where it's going." I psychically saw a circle of women, all of them dressed in black and with a large Christian cross over the front of each of them. One of my books was in the center of their circle and they were directing energy into it. The energy felt like hate, and I became nauseous—as nauseous as I had been on the lecture tour. "They know exactly what they're doing and they're doing it with intent," the healer said. "They keep renewing it, too."

I did not have the methods of working with the Lords of Karma then, so the healer called upon Archangel Michael, possibly my first time meeting him. I asked that the arrow be removed and the women's curses and attacks ended. We watched the string being cut from the end of the arrow and the arrow itself taken from my energy. The nausea increased and I nearly vomited. The healer asked that Michael clean up the mess, and the Light from his sword entered my abdomen to sterilize the pus and infection. For the next several days I was nauseous and felt ripped open, but the years of unexplained weakness quickly changed and healed. The healer said, and she could not have known this, "they were praying for you to die."

Years later still, when working with the Lords of Karma to clear all negative relationships, the Christian women came to mind again. I asked for karmic release, healing, and severance from them and all their kind. I was shown then that they were the source of my many years of vision difficulties. Besides the three who came to the lectures and the circle that I saw, many of their friends joined them in praying against me. I asked for release from the situation and karmic severance from all the perpetrators. As they were Earth karma only, I did not need (and did not yet know) Divine Director, though I confirmed that later. The vision of Archangel Michael in that healing remains to this day; I had never seen an angel before, and never before had one come to my assistance and aid.

Perhaps what these women were doing was not prayer, but cursing, negative ritual, and psychic attack. Prayer is energy used for good, just as psychic healing is. It is meant for blessing, not cursing. Ritual is meant to be used for blessing and good, as well. Similar Christians' prayers requesting that someone gay be made straight is also a form of curse. Nothing that Christ ever taught in his lifetime or later in Christianity ever promoted such negative or manipulative use of energy. Such actions are not the right use of any religion, they come from hatred and they are evil.

The attacks originated in this lifetime. If they had not been discovered and removed in this lifetime, they would have continued to blight my current life and been carried forward into other incarnations. With each incarnation, the damage would have continued and increased, and I would likely be attacked again by the same women or their group. Discovering what happened, removing the energy, and ending the karma will prevent it from replicating into other lifetimes.

Such misuse of energy can be taken too lightly in our current culture. Today's psychics and Women's Spirituality witches often refuse to take hexing, curses, psychic attacks, and their like seriously. Possibly people in a modern age refuse to believe in the reality of "bad thoughts." Possibly people are afraid to acknowledge that anyone would really do such things, or would do such things to them. Maybe the whole idea is just too scary, and denying it gives people the excuse not to deal with it. Yet these things are all around us. Metaphysical magazines and botanicas offer charms and spells for just about everything, talismans, charged candles, and other objects, gris-gris bags. We even have a classic pop song about "Love Potion Number Nine," and there are lots of purported-to-be-old spell books available.

All of this is playing with fire.

Love spells are classic examples, and I've touched upon these before. A friend of mine experienced a rather involved one and we worked together with the Lords of Karma to clear it. She had never been able to get pregnant by her husband, though when she was younger she very much wanted a child. She experienced serious flooding and bleeding with each menstrual cycle, something she had always had and always taken for granted. First, we discovered a vow that she had made early on to only have children with a particular partner, an old flame just coming back into her life. (I will call him Rich, and call her ex-husband John.) Next, we discovered from the Lords of Karma that she was unable to get pregnant because her monthly menstrual flooding was a monthly miscarriage.

The situation came from a past life. She was a servant in a castle and a higher-born man (her former husband John in this life) wanted her sexually. He obtained a love spell from someone in the castle and used the woman sexually, the spell making her accept and want him, though she did not love him. John didn't want the complication of her becoming pregnant, so from the same person who made the love spell he obtained a poison. The poison placed in her drink made her miscarry, and he made sure she took it often enough. Rich was engaged to the woman in that life, but John threatened to kill him if he approached her. In the present lifetime, Rich was the woman's first love, but the early relationship didn't work out. She swore she would have children only with Rich but married John instead and had no children with him. The love spell placed by John in the past life was still in effect, and so was his poisoning of her.

After receiving this information from the Lords of Karma, we asked them to remove the love spells and end the effects of the poison. We also asked them to cancel the karma of John's threats which were preventing Rich from marrying her. The vow to have children only with Rich has been cancelled, as well. The woman is now with her first love. I warned her to be aware of birth control, since she no longer wants children and could get pregnant. We are discussing herbs to heal the excessive menstrual bleeding. She has decided to cancel all karma and karmic contracts with John.

Since people tend to reincarnate in groups, I was not surprised to discover another friend who was poisoned in the same past life by the same poisoner. She had experienced severe gastric attacks for most of her adulthood, but no physical cause for them had ever been found. She had gone to the Lords of Karma a number of times for help, and though the condition had lessened in frequency and force it still occurred. Not long after dealing with the last woman's karma of poisoning, someone suggested that these gastric attacks also sounded like poison. We went to the Lords of Karma and Divine Director and asked about it. The woman had indeed died of poisoning, murdered by the same person who provided the spells and poison against our other friend. We asked to cancel all karma and all karmic contracts with the poisoner and to end her curses, attacks, and poisoning forever on all of our group of friends. The woman with the gastric attacks is regaining her health.

In a past life of my own, I was killed by an obsidian ax that had been poisoned and negatively charged to cause harm that would never heal. I died from the ax wound the first time and have been killed by the same ax in several other past lives. For about two years my psychic abilities were blocked by what I perceived as an object in the center part of my head. Several people told me it was an ax blade but as often as I asked to remove it, it kept coming back. I also perceived what seemed to be a piece of ragged black metal shaped something like a lightning bolt, below or under the ax blade. It took putting the two together to find the source and end the obstruction. The ax blade had been spelled and the metal object was the mechanism (perhaps a symbol used for harm) of the spell itself. Only after I made the connection between the two objects, asking to remove at the source both the ax and the spell that was connected to it, did the Lords of Karma and Divine Director release the karma and the spell. The objects dissolved and my psychic abilities were free to operate again.

Symbols are psychic mechanisms. They can be mechanisms for great good, as in the case of the Reiki symbols, or they can be abused and used as weapons for great harm. The Christian Cross is probably the symbol most often called upon for both harm and good. The five Reiki symbols, at least, are protected so that they cannot be used for negative interference. Most other symbols are not so well protected. People constantly present me with what they think are the "lost" Reiki symbols; they are usually healing symbols from other traditions or systems which may be positive in themselves, but some of them are not positive or can be misused.

In one case, I showed a sheet of these supposed Reiki symbols to a woman of my acquaintance. She decided that one of them, which looked like a pyramid with a cross on the top, was a protection symbol and she began using it on everyone and everything around her. When she tried it on me, it immediately felt wrong, and I asked her to take it off and not to use it again. She refused to remove the symbol and continued to send it at me. Again, this was before I knew the Lords of Karma, and though I asked repeatedly for help in removing the symbol it remained. I felt as though I was trapped inside a stifling bell jar. The air felt stagnant and became more and more negative and toxic. Feeling imprisoned, first I became extremely restless and then panicked. This went on over a two-day period. I asked the woman again to remove the symbols, but this time she insisted that there were none.

I called upon the Light again and again, but though I felt things shift, it wasn't enough. I tried Reiki symbols next. The Sei-Hei-Kei should have worked, but didn't. I felt more and more suffocated, more panicky, and felt I was struggling for my life. Eventually, with the help of the Reiki Raku symbol and the added strength of another healer, I removed the pyramid. We then discovered that there were layers of pyramids, sent in waves repeatedly to surround my energy, my house, even my dogs. The pyramids had the effect of enclosing energy without an opening for release or escape. The effect was suffocating indeed.

Years later, working with the Lords of Karma I asked about the black pyramids. I was shown that there were still more of them surrounding my aura and the aura of one of my dogs. I asked that they be removed at the source; I had long since asked for karmic severance with the woman. Later still, working with Divine Director I found much more interference from this woman, who has attacked me through many planets and life-times. A major piece of the Negative Form was inhabiting her and working through her, hosting it by her own choice. Anything she sent against me gained the force of the Negative Form evil working through her. Because of the entity, every-thing she sent became much worse than what she had the strength to do on her own.

When I learned about karmic contracts, I asked to cancel all karma and all karmic contracts with this person, and I was shown more from the current lifetime. The woman had taught a negative spell to a developmentally disabled woman of her acquaintance. She told her that to do this ritual would heal me and, not comprehending, the woman did it faithfully every month for years. The ritual was a spell designed to blind me. In it she had the woman place "herbs" on my eyes and Third Eye with the intent of burning and poisoning them. I had been experiencing significant burning and discomfort in my eyes for a long time and thought it was an allergic reaction. Once this incident was cleared—I had to clear the karma with both women, plus their spells and rituals, as well as all karma with the damage—the burning went away. Fully clearing my karma with this woman has been a ten-year process, hopefully now complete.

Like symbols, objects positive in themselves can also be used for harm. Anything that carries energy can be used or abused, though energy is a neutral thing. I believe energy to be intrinsically good, and that all but a very few people are intrinsically good, but energy can still be misused and people can do wrong. Electricity is a form of energy—it can be used to light your home or burn it down. As for crystals, I have loved them all my life and probably over many lifetimes, but they have been used to transmit psychic attacks to harm me and to harm others. In one case, a crystal that sits on a table in my living room was programmed by someone of ill intent. She used it as a focus to enter my living space and attacked me through it. I have asked the Lords of Karma and Divine Director to seal my home and all the objects in it, including all my crystals, against evil.

Thought is also a neutral force that can be used to carry good or harm. Mental focus amplifies and transmits energy, as crystals amplify and transmit energy. Any focused thought can be used to transmit harm as well as good. It works more easily in this modern day because unlike past times, people today choose not to believe that psychic attacks or spells are real. Energy can be programmed by thought, the same way a computer can be programmed to do anything you want it to do. I wrote previously about the unwisdom of letting your mind create worst-case scenarios. Worst-case scenarios can be programmed into your energy by someone else. This is mental manipulation, a spell, or a psychic attack. It is against all human and karmic ethics. Remember that what you do has karmic consequences; the people who do such manipulation will be dealt with.

Since returning negative energy and attacks to their senders is not the way to do it, how can we protect ourselves? When we trade attack for attack we start a psychic war that causes harm to all, psychically and karmically. The processes of this book so far will provide you with the foundation for protection from these attacks. So is the awareness that such things exist and are real. If you have removed all your negative hooks and cords, you have probably cancelled your karma with more than one person who negatively manipulated or attacked you. Next you must make a direct request to end all such manipulation and deliberate interference with your energy from all your lifetimes.

To do this, go into your meditative space and ask to speak with the Lords of Karma and Divine Director. Ask them to cancel all your karma and karmic contracts from Earth and all other planets with all negative spells, rituals, curses, symbols (including positive symbols used in negative ways), and enchantments. Take this through the full Earth karmic release process, plus the process for clearing off-planet karma. Next ask to cancel all karma and all karmic contracts with all perpetrators of these negative manipulations—these are not people you want to keep in your life for this or any other lifetime. Again, use both karmic release processes. With both of these requests pay careful attention to the information or pictures you are shown.

Next, ask the Lords of Karma and Divine Director to cancel all karma and all karmic contracts with all damage and all replication of damage from spells, rituals, curses, symbols, and enchantments. Ask to cancel all karma and all karmic contracts with all negative effects from all forms of interference through all your lifetimes on all planets—and between them. Ask to heal and regenerate your energy of all damage, including replacing any components that are too damaged to be easily healed. Ask to purify your energy—through all the levels and components of your Be-ing, all dimensions, all connections, and all systems and between them—of all negative interference energies and their effects. Ask to cancel all karma and all karmic contracts forever with all types and all incidences of negative interference to your energy and your life, and with all their sources and perpetrators. With each of these requests use both karmic release processes, the one for clearing Earth karma and the one for off-planet lifetimes.

Take time to do these processes slowly. If you are shown information about any particular lifetime or situation, it is important to pay attention to it. With any situation you are shown, ask if you need to do a separate release process for that specific situation or with the person involved. If so, make it another full karmic release request, using the Earth and off-planet processes. If you are shown a person who has deliberately tried to harm you, also ask to cancel all karma and karmic contracts specifically with that person, whether you know them in this life or not. The karma of deliberate interference has the nasty habit of returning over many lifetimes. If someone has deliberately attacked you, manipulated you, or used spells against you, request the end of all karma and all karmic contracts with them forever.

You may be amazed and shocked at what you are shown. I knew that the woman of the black pyramids was doing evil things, but I charitably chalked it up to ignorance when it was not. I was shown lifetime after lifetime in which she had done similar wrongs, and several in which she had deliberately engineered my death or the deaths of those I loved. I found that anyone who was attacking me energetically now had done so many times before. Women talk about breaking the chain of abuse, and this is as good an example of it as I can think of. This is a karmic chain you wish to end irrevocably without ever looking back. Just be certain you understand what you see and what you are to do. If in doubt, ask the Lords of Karma and Divine Director for fuller information. A pendulum that swings yes or no can give you a yes or no answer to whether a particular person has done you harm. You can use it to determine whether or not it is appropriate to cancel all your karma and karmic contracts with them.

In another process, ask the Lords of Karma and Divine Director to cancel all karma and all karmic contracts with all negative past life artifacts, and to remove them forever from your energy. Artifacts are objects that have had power for you in this or other lifetimes. I wear a turquoise chunk necklace that was a power object for me when I was a Native American midwife and shaman many lifetimes ago. This is a positive artifact, but many such objects can be negative. A less positive one that was removed from me in a healing, was a beautiful gold and faceted ruby necklace, probably a very expensive one. In that lifetime in Russia I was a wealthy and frustrated wife, forced to be an ornament and not permitted any independence. The necklace was a symbol of my frustration.

I have removed hanging ropes from a number of people's necks during healings, like the ax blade, and a variety of other weapons. If such objects have been spelled, or used in negative rituals, spells, or other interference, they can carry ongoing damage and harm. When you make the request to clear all negative artifacts from your energy, you may be shown several such items. If you want to know more, you may have to ask. If they come up in your meditation as a result of your request, just ask that they be removed. Ask if there are spells to remove from any of them, and make sure all negative spells on these objects are cancelled.

Ask that all such artifacts and objects be "annihilated, extinguished, uncreated, and obliterated forever," as they carry energies you will not wish returned to you at any time. Once the objects are removed and "annihilated," ask that all damage from them be regenerated and healed, and all negative effects removed, with any components too damaged to heal being fully replaced. Ask that all replication of these objects or their negative effects in your energy be ended forever. All of these requests are individual Lords of Karma and Divine Director processes, and all are best done using both the Earth and other-planet releases. If this work takes a few nights' meditations to complete, that is fine. However, since if any of these are off-planet karma their clearing will result in the closing up of your Crown for a few hours, you may wish to do as many at one time as you can. Most of them, however, will be from Earth.

Once you have done the above and feel reasonably sure you have seen all the incidents of negative interference and psychic abuse and attack in your lifetimes, it is time to make requests that will prevent further such karmas from forming. Ask the Lords of Karma and Divine Director to raise your energy vibration beyond the point where negative interference and negative spells, curses, rituals, symbols, and enchantments can reach or harm you. Ask that this raising of your vibration be permanent and forever, and protected from being pulled down or lowered for any reason. This is similar to raising your energy above the negative mass consciousness, but you must raise your vibration considerably higher to achieve this. Again use both the Earth and other-planet karmic release process for this request, and do both full processes. You may ask to protect your home, garden, family, and pets in this way, as well.

If at this point your energy has not been totally cleared of negative interference, the raising of your vibration will complete the clearing. In the next several days you may see new incidents of what seem to be attacks on your energy. You have shaken the rug and the bugs are flying out. Go to the Lords of Karma and Divine Director to cancel all karma and all karmic contracts with whatever you see—whether you understand it or not. If you feel you are being attacked, call upon Archangel Michael (for Earth karma) or Archangel Ashtar (for off-planet karma) to clear and do battle with the negatives you see. These things will disappear and be fully cleared in a few days. Again, consider them pain leaving you.

When these processes are complete and your energy is raised, you will not be subject to psychic attacks or spells again.

9

NONHUMAN INTERFERENCE

Not all negative interference and energy attacks are from human sources, though the majority of them are. There are also energies that are nonliving, nonhuman, mindless, and without souls. In a way, these are easier to deal with since there is no ethic against destroying them, as there is for anything containing life. But they are also very foreign to human ways of thinking and understanding, and this can make them a different sort of challenge. While you are not dealing with human hate here, you may be dealing with something that has no concept of love. It also may have no sense of place or dimension.

Some interference from human sources can also be from imprints of people who have long since died. You never knew these people and have no karma with them, but they may blunder into your environment or awareness. Negative entities, human or not, can inhabit—possess—human energy and must be cleared. A further type of interference comes, strangely enough, from damaged fragments of our own personalities and souls.

Attachments are nonhuman energies that inhabit and possess living people. Some of them have a job to do, as they are manifestations of karmic contracts for dis-eases or for karmic restrictions to your life or life purpose. They incarnate with you or can be connected to your energy later. In every case, what they do in your energy is negative and harmful in some way. They may originate on Earth or on other planets, or enter your energy in the between life state. They are other-dimensional, having reality and existence on a different dimension from our third dimensional physical Be-ings. They are not alive or comprised of living components; they have never been alive.

These things surface frequently in healing sessions, and a clearing of attachments can make major changes in a person's life. They are nothing to fight, they are not alive—just energy that is there. To someone who sees psychically, they may appear as blobs of tarry substance or have nonhuman forms. They may appear as unearthly monsters or demons of strange shape. These are different from the implant projections we will discuss in the next chapter. Attachments will usually not appear as infestations of bugs, rats, or snakes, but are things not usually seen on Earth. To describe them as cartoon figures or caricatures probably comes the closest.

It's disconcerting to be doing a healing and watch some small blue man with a large nose surface in a person's energy or surface from a chakra. These things are not attacks, they have not been sent by anyone, they just appear. They seem to have no plausible origin or reason for being there. Upon observing such a phenomenon, try to make psychic contact with it. Ask it why it's there, what it's doing in the person's energy. Ask it what's its job. After questioning a number of such things over a period of years, they all have a similar story. The attachment is there to create a dis-ease or discomfort for the person. It has no idea why or how it arrived there, it's always been there, and it will always be there until its job is done. When asked if it understands that it's causing harm or suffering, these Be-ings have no idea what suffering is. They mean no harm. Being there is just their job.

Once you know what its job is, you have a place to start. There's no point in yelling at the creature, it has no idea why you're angry. When you find out what its job is, you need to end it. This can be done by calling in the Lords of Karma and Divine Director and asking to end the person's karma and karmic contracts with the "job." For example, if the attachment is there to maintain a tumor, request to end all karma and all karmic contracts with the tumor. Make sure you end the tumor's source and the karma's source from Earth and all other planets, as well. As soon as the release is granted, return to the attachment and tell it, "Your job is done, you've done well but now it's finished. Now you can return to the Light."

Tell the attachment it must go "home." Assure it that it will not be punished for its work, but welcomed and healed. If it argues or refuses, ask for the Angels of Blue Lightning or any other angel of the Light to come and take it where it needs to be. Use Reiki Raku symbols. You will see the open door, similar to what you saw in passing over ghosts. Make sure it passes fully through the door, and this time, make sure the door is barred and locked afterwards. If there is difficulty, go back to the Lords of Karma and Divine Director and ask that the attachment be removed forever, never to return.

Once this is done, check the person's energy for more attachments, because where there is one, there can be many. You may ask the Lords of Karma and Divine Director to cancel all karma and all karmic contracts with all energy attachments, at their sources, from Earth and all other planets and between them. You may then have several such creatures to send to the Light. Make sure they all go. Ask that all damage and harm done by all attachments be fully healed, and the person's entire energy fully purified. Ask for full healing and regeneration, with any components replaced that are too damaged to heal. Make sure these healings include the physical body. Ask for gentle and easy integration once all attachments are gone and their damage has been repaired.

Now that you have done this in a healing session for someone else, make the same requests for yourself. Ask the Lords of Karma and Divine Director to cancel all karma and all karmic contracts, from Earth and all other planets, with all energy attachments—and with all harm and damage they have caused. Ask that all attachments be taken to the Light and never permitted to return to you. Ask for total healing as you did above. Do both the Earth and off-planet karmic release processes for these clearings. Some very stubborn dis-eases may leave with the strange little characters. Sometimes asking for the karmic release of a dis-ease causes one or more of these attachments to leave on its own.

Sometimes attachments have no perceivable form, or have not displayed their form to your psychic vision. They seem a mass of jelly in someone's energy or your own, or simply something you know is negative. Ask the Lords of Karma and Divine Director to remove the negative energy at its source and both the source and the harm the energy is causing. Ask to cancel all karma and all karmic contracts with both the attachment and the attachment's source. You don't have to understand what these things are in order to ask for them. You may or may not be shown, and the energy and its source may or may not be from Earth.

Once your requests are granted, the attachment should begin to leave. If it does not, call upon the Angels of Blue Lightning or any angel of the Light to remove it. All angels seem to delight in fighting this kind of negative energy. Use Reiki Raku symbols. Ask if the attachment is to be passed over (or under), or if it is to be annihilated. By the time your healing is finished these attachments should be removed and you should know where they have gone. Don't just ask to send them away. If they are to pass over, you want to see them gone and the door locked. If they are to pass under, you want to see them safely immersed in the white flames of the Fire of Life at the Center of the Earth. If they are to be destroyed, make sure it is done. These energies can be slippery and you don't want them coming back to reattach to you, or to harm someone else.

A pain trap is a situation that resembles an attachment but is somewhat different. I had what I assumed to be a karmic pattern of never seeming to be able to reach success. Every time I was on the upward path and the breakthrough was the next step, something always seemed to push me back to the bottom. It happened so many times that it became a disheartening way to live. The pattern appeared in my finances, my writing, my relationships—in every aspect of my life. This was before I knew about the Lords of Karma, so I asked a friend for a healing session to help me find the source. We found in my energy a strange-looking little man, standing on a wheel-type mechanism that looked like a phonograph record. His job was to keep me at the bottom and he was succeeding. We removed him from my energy, but I had a sense that he wasn't gone. I found him on several more energy levels in the next few days and removed him from those.

Years later in working with Divine Director and the Lords of Karma, I happened to ask about the pain trap and found that he was still there. I was told that he was neither an attachment, a past life, nor a karmic pattern, and that he was not from Earth. He was also not and had never been a living Be-ing. I asked to cancel all karma and all karmic contracts with him and was told that it was now complete. He was not to be passed over or under, or annihilated—just to be removed. My suggestion is to go to the Lords of Karma and Divine Director and ask if such pain traps exist in your energy. If they do, use the off-planet process to clear them—they are not and will never be Earth energy.

Another version of nonhuman energy is the negative elemental. These are nonliving manifestations of Earth, Air, Fire, Water, or Metal. They have no consciousness, but they have great force and power—generally destructive power. They can attach to human energy. During one very chaotic period of my life I was told I had a tornado attached to my aura. Images from *The Wizard of Oz* kept coming up in healings. The healer and I laughed about the images, but it was a long time until we really got the message. Finally when we asked to release the tornado, things in my life calmed down considerably. With an elemental, you don't turn it loose and you don't pass it over. You must make very sure that it isn't set free to harm anyone else. These things have such force that I suspect an unsupervised one could do great harm, maybe even become a manifested tornado or hurricane.

I have no idea how these things form, or why. I do know, however, they are not evil in themselves, but are only energy occurring in the wrong place. They are like the proverbial bull in the china shop. Where a bull in the pasture is positive, out of its right place it causes havoc. This is what happens with a negative elemental. In another version of nonhuman energy, what I thought was a pine tree deva in my yard was instead a negative fire elemental. Its penchant for disruption appeared in appliances and electricity, with a steady parade of blown fuses, burned out light bulbs, and failing kitchen equipment. After the automatic garage door fell on me, I was told it was too dangerous to approach the entity, I was simply to move out of the house. I contacted the Lords of Karma before I did, asking that the elemental not move with me. Once in my new home, I requested that the elemental be taken care of safely, and it was.

An elemental needs to be passed under, rather than over. It must go to the Fire of Life at the core of the Earth for recycling. These are dangerous forces of nature, out of their proper place and out of control. Call upon the Lords of Karma to deal with them; they are not only of Earth origin. Ask to cancel all karma and all karmic contracts with them, and ask that they be removed safely and placed in the Fire of Life for purification. Ask that all damage they have done be regenerated and healed on all levels and through all systems. This includes damage to you, to all other people and Be-ings, and to the Earth. I suspect that negative elementals are the cause of some severe weather aberrations we are experiencing with the Earth changes. Planetary chaos either creates them or shifts them from where they are supposed to be. They are not formed by negative interference or by human will.

The human and once-living variety of attachment is called a possession. This is when someone dies and refuses to pass over, and then attaches themselves to and inhabits the energy of a living person. The person that is possessed is usually vulnerable in some way, with aura weakness or damage that the ghost can easily breach. Children can be vulnerable. Healthy adults with strong auras are not easily subject to possession. Most possessions happen in hospitals or funeral homes, or at the scenes of accidents. The person usually dies suddenly, does not want to die, and is frantic to remain. He or she finds someone nearby who is available and vulnerable, and enters that person. There is usually some amount of sympathy or unconscious agreement on the part of the person possessed. The one who died may have been a relative or loved one, or the person receiving the possession has pity for the person who died suddenly.

145

After years of energy clearing and working with the Lords of Karma I happened to ask to be cleared of all possessions. I was reading a book on the subject and just thought I'd check it out. I didn't expect to find anything. Yet something was there, and though I didn't get a look at it, I felt it leave. I had a sense of great relief when it did. I was told that it had done no damage, had been there since childhood, and was someone I had never met. I had no real karma with it and it did not mean me harm. It was a woman, and I made sure she was fully passed over. Any spirit that does not leave the Earth after death does not receive the after-life healing it requires, and it cannot reincarnate.

The other experience I had with possession was not this benign. During a workshop several years ago, a woman asked me to do healing for her child, a four-year-old boy who was manifesting symptoms of mental and emotional disturbance. The mother didn't know what was wrong and asked for help. When I was introduced to him, I did not see a small child, but a middle-aged man. He was short and stocky, with grey crew-cut hair; his arms were folded belligerently over his chest, and he was spoiling for a fight. I told the mother what I saw, and she said, "Oh my gosh, that's his grandfather." The grandfather had died when the child was eight months old. He had not been a pleasant man.

I asked the boy if I could touch him to do healing. When he agreed, I put my hands on him. As soon as I did, the child exploded into torrents of verbal abuse, calling me names that no four year old should ever know, and he began kicking and punching. He ran away into the front yard where his mother and another woman restrained him. He was kicking, thrashing, and screaming. I had never seen a possession before, but knew that's what I was dealing with. The grandfather was in the child's body;

I didn't know where the child was. I called the grandfather's name and told him he was dead and that he had to leave.

The thrashing and screaming increased. I called for the old man's angels and spirit guides to come and take him over. The man in the boy's body yelled and threatened and said he wasn't leaving. I argued and fought with him for some time. I didn't have the benefit of the Lords of Karma's help then, but I needed it badly. My Goddess Brede was there, but unable to help because of the negativity. The entity attacked me, beating against my energy in an attempt to harm me or come in. I ordered him away and started sending Reiki Raku symbols. He finally moved away from me, and an angel took the man away.

Once the grandfather was gone, I went back to the little boy, now lying quietly on the ground. All the kicking and thrashing had stopped, but he was unresponsive. His mother leaned over him, calling his name, but with the grandfather gone, there was no one in the body. I appealed to Brede, who now could help, and she showed me the child's spirit. He was curled up in a fetal position about two feet above his physical form. The vision I saw was of a baby, much younger than the boy's current age. Brede brought the baby into the child's body and the boy sat up. He sucked his thumb and asked for his mother. Brede told me that it would take him a month to grow back to his chronological age and to tell his mother to give him lots of love and not to be afraid.

The entity came into the child at his death when the boy was eight months old. It happened at the funeral; the baby was there because the mother couldn't find a babysitter. The grandfather was strong and mean, and he didn't want to pass over; the infant was vulnerable. There was apparently some karmic contract between the grandfather and the child. In the days following the dispossession, the boy drew Raku after Raku with his crayons and wanted to be rocked. A few months later, the grandfather returned and entered again, but the mother chased him off. This time she sealed his energy unto the Light, and the grandfather never tried again. The child had no more bouts of violent or disturbed behavior from that day on. He had been having them frequently and regularly before he was brought to me for the healing. Today he is a fully normal child. It was one of the most intense and frightening healings I have ever done or witnessed.

There are easier ways to do a dispossession, of course. Go to the Lords of Karma and Divine Director and ask that all possessions be removed and passed over. Ask that all karma and all karmic contracts with possession and with the possessing spirits be ended forever. Ask that all the damage be fully healed. You can do this in a psychic distance healing or directly if necessary. It is a gentler, more civilized way. I recommend asking this for yourself too and checking to see if any possession entities are there. They will clear easily with the Lords of Karma and Divine Director's help, with just the simple requests. In the case of the child and his grandfather, I wish I had known then what I know now.

Something resembling an entity or a possession can happen when part of your own personality splits off. A soul split is more than a soul fragment or a subpersonality, as the part is fully developed but unknown to the person carrying it. It is a separate personality that can wreak havoc. It is not a multiple personality, which makes itself known, but very close. I have seen these twice, once in myself and once in someone else. In both cases, the request had long since been made to "heal, bring in, and fully integrate all soul fragments from all lifetimes and planets." Make this request to the Lords of Karma and Divine Director now, if you haven't done so already and use the full Earth process. But a soul fragment and soul split are not the same.

Soul fragments occur at times of trauma, fear, or great emotional pain. If the shock is strong enough, the Astral Twin/Inner Child can suffer damage or break apart. Fragments that are holograms of the Astral Twin separate and float free. These look like the whole Be-ing, but will remain the age and appearance at the time when the fragmentation occurred. The breaking off of a soul fragment makes the person feel spacey, disconnected, emotionally numb, disinterested in life, and not all there. With the many incarnations we have experienced and the many traumas incurred in them, the Astral Twin can be fragmented again and again until it is in many pieces. Each fragmenting leaves the Emotional Body a little more damaged and a little more vulnerable to further damage. There may be dozens of soul fragments from many lifetimes on Earth or from other planets. The above request to the Lords of Karma and Divine Director heals and returns these fragments gently. This is a standard Essential Energy Balancing request. The process takes a few weeks to complete and it's a pleasant process. I had done this long ago.

In my experience with the personality split, I had a recurring bad habit of becoming upset with some strangers and yelling and getting very nasty with them. These were usually shopkeepers or repairmen who frustrated me, never people I knew or was close to. I was ashamed of my aggressive stance with them. Each time it happened I felt horribly guilty and didn't understand why it had occurred. It was a character trait I wanted cleared and went to the Lords of Karma for help, but the situation didn't seem to get any better. People used to tease me about my "Evil Twin," and like the tornado it took me awhile to catch on.

One day in sheer frustration I asked the Lords of Karma to heal the "Evil Twin" or get rid of her. They told me she couldn't be healed. I asked what I should do and if I was on the right track. They told me she had to be removed and passed over. They added that she was neither a soul fragment, nor a multiple personality, nor a subpersonality but a full personality of her own while still a part of me. When I asked if passing her over was for my best good and the good of all, they said it was. I then asked for it, though I was uneasy about the whole idea. I requested they show me my "Evil Twin" leaving, still not understanding what it was. Almost as soon as I made the request I saw an image of myself at about two years old, determined, angry little girl in red corduroy overalls and white blouse with ruffled sleeves. I was carrying a blue suitcase, large for my size, and trudged with it, unescorted, through the open golden door. The door closed, and all I felt was great relief. I never had an incident of yelling at shop people again, and much of my residual anger and frustration went with it.

In another case of an "Evil Twin," a woman in one of my workshops received a no to every Lords of Karma request she made. She disrupted the workshop and made the other women very angry, but I had a sense that something was really wrong and needed healing. I thought she had an entity or an attachment and told her to make the request to remove them. The "Gremlin" as we called it, quieted down and I thought it was gone. The next morning it came to visit me in bed, and out of patience I told it that it had two choices. It could either leave Earth forever and go back to where it originated, or I would annihilate it. It left in a hurry.

Some months later, the woman confessed that the "Gremlin" was still around saying no to everything. I couldn't understand why it had come back, or why it was still there. Finally, it occurred to me to have the woman ask the Lords of Karma if it was like my "Evil Twin." It was. We asked again about its nature—if it was a multiple personality, a subpersonality, or a soul fragment, but were told it was none of these. The only explanation I was given for the phenomenon was the "soul split" term. We were told that the "Gremlin" had to be passed over and the woman made the request. Hopefully, the "Gremlin" is gone forever, like my "Evil Twin." While I don't feel many people will have one of these, it is probably good to ask the Lords of Karma and Divine Director if any soul splits exist in your energy. If they tell you yes, ask to cancel all karma and karmic contracts with it and ask to pass it over. Soul splits can be caused by attacks to your energy.

One last type of nonhuman manifestation is the energy imprint. These are leftovers of things that have already been cleared and removed. You are told by the Lords of Karma and Divine Director that something is done and it's gone, but you still perceive that it's there. You see it, hear it, and feel it, and the situation continues. You think it's still attacking you, but it is not. These are similar to dreams, but are usually experienced while you are awake. They are energy repeats, working through the layers to dissolve.

On a number of occasions I was awakened suddenly, fighting what seemed to be attacks. The attacking entities were things I'd previously removed, or similar, and I thought they had come back. When I went rushing to the Lords of Karma for help, their attitude was ho-hum, almost bored. "Done," they said to every request; "It's done." When I called for Archangel Michael to annihilate the attacking entities, I received the same response. Usually, if I feel that something is attacking me it really is, and I wondered what this was about. Apparently, after something clears it can leave this imprint behind. In moving through the energy levels for clearing, the imprint can take longer to clear than the thing itself. I assumed this was something mental but was told it was not, and I was assured that it was not a dream. Just more pain leaving, I supposed.

There is an another entity phenomenon that was shown to me to explain these imprints. If you have ever visited a battlefield, and checked into it psychically, you will receive a very realistic vision of the battle still being fought. On many occasions I have attempted to pass over the people I saw fighting and dying on battlefields from wars of long ago. I thought I saw the Beings pass over, but the next time I looked at the battle site in Gettysburg the war was still going on. I suspect that such imprints are emotional and are the result of leftover fear. They happen when there is intense emotion both physical and psychic, evident at the point when physical (the war) and psychic (the passing over) come together.

When I thought I was still being attacked, I had great emotional intensity with the situations when they were happening. There was an element of fear, as well. The combination, along with strong desire to not be attacked again, combined to create an imprint of what had already ended. In the case of the battlefield, the war had been over for more than a hundred years. A great many psychics had tried their hand for many years at passing over the many dead. The great fear of the men who died remained, however, as did mine from the attacks and the fear created both imprints. When I understood that the images I was seeing were no longer there, I simply asked the Lords of Karma and Divine Director to erase the imprints of what was no longer real.

The best way to prevent entities, attachments, elementals, pain traps, possessions, and other negative energies from reaching and affecting you, is to first clear your karma of them. If you have followed along with the material in this chapter you have already done this each step of the way. Whenever anything strange and negative comes along, ask first if you need clearing from it. Is it from Earth or some other planet (or between them)? Is the energy living or nonliving, human or not? Is it karmic? Ask if it's something you need to be concerned about. By now you have enough contact with the Lords of Karma or your Guardian Angel, your Goddess, or other Be-ings of the Light to ask questions and get answers. Ask what that something is, ask if something needs to be done about it, and ask what you should do.

As a next step, once you've cleared your karma of the incident or energy, ask that it be removed forever. Is it to be passed over or passed under? Is it to be destroyed? I like the term "annihilated," something to be done only to nonliving negative energy. You may also ask that this nonliving negative energy be "annihilated, extinguished, uncreated, and obliterated forever." That should finish it! If none of these things is to be done, ask for further instructions. It may need only to be removed; it may need to be sent "home," wherever its home may be. The Lords of Karma can help you understand what needs to be done, but they will expect you then to make the request for them to do so. Never ask to destroy any living Be-ing or living energy, no matter how evil it may seem, unless the Lords of Karma tell you to do so.

Next, ask that all damage from the negativity be healed and, if necessary, all your karma and karmic contracts with the damage be cancelled. Healing all damage means more than asking for healing. Ask for healing and regeneration, and ask to replace any components that are too damaged to be easily healed. Sometimes it is easier for the Lords of Karma and the Light to replace something than to repair it. New chakras can be screwed in like changing a light bulb. If they tell you something can't be repaired, don't despair. Along with healing, ask that the energy be returned to full purity with all replication of evil ended and removed. This can be important if an attachment or attack is an energy that reincarnates with you. Ask that all components and systems be brought back to full and optimal function. In my attempt to find one phrase that means "fix everything," "all systems" seems to come closest.

Ask that your energy be made invulnerable to this type of interference and all negative interference forever. This usually means requesting that your vibrational level be raised beyond the point where the interference can reach you. There is always a level of Light beyond which you cannot be attacked. By asking to clear, heal, reconnect, and fully activate the full complement of your DNA, you will automatically and eventually be brought to that point.

The next chapter discusses past life karma from other planets.

10

OTHER PLANET KARMA

Earth is the focus of a great deal of interplanetary and intergalactic attention at this time. We are at a point of major planetary growth and development, a point of do or die. We have taken the steps to bring this planet to Ascension and the Light. It was not always assured that we could achieve this. I am told that the decision *not* to destroy this planet was made only in the last ten years. Earth has been the object of interplanetary war since its creation. We have been taken over by many forms and manifestations of evil. This is not to say that most people are evil, though some have allowed themselves to be used by evil. At this time in the Earth changes, we are in an intensive process of clearing and transformation, a process that will give us back our freedom and return us to the Light.

Many other-planetary Be-ings of the Light are assisting Earth and Earth people. Our evolutionary roots are primarily from the Pleiades, and the Pleiadian Federation is at the forefront of those protecting and helping us. Many of the most positive technological advances that help to preserve the environment and ecology, improve the practice of medicine, and find alternative forms of energy have come from Pleiadian sources. Many scientists on Earth in increasing numbers starting with Einstein and Tesla have channeled information from the stars. Many forces of the

Light from other planets and galaxies are fighting the wars that will free us from domination and evil.

Other-planetary help is bringing new information to Earth in a variety of subjects and skills. We are no longer quarantined in the Universe, as we were until recently. The decision then was to wait and see if we would become Light or accept the dominance of the negative dark. There was much of the negative dark on Earth. We were left to make our own choices, to evolve or end the Earth, to choose war, genocide, racism, planetary destruction, and hatred—or to reject them. There is now a critical mass of people rejecting wrong and determined to create positive change. We are granted all the help that we need. The wars for our freedom are almost finished, and we will prevail in the Light.

We live in exciting times. There is a Chinese curse that says, "May you live in interesting times," and these times go far beyond interesting. It is not a peaceful or complacent time to be alive. Our planet is a whirling vortex of transformational change. Nothing is stagnant any longer on Earth, and the changes are happening too fast for comfort. However, these changes are needed if we are to continue to exist at all. We have waited for them for many thousands of years and wondered if they would ever come. In an earlier Earth change prophecy, we were told that the planet would be destroyed and that ships would come to remove good Be-ings at the end. The current plan is to ascend the planet and everyone on it, a far more positive scene. No one will be destroyed. We are in a process of doing just that, ascending people and the planet as a whole.

To achieve Ascension for an individual person or the Earth itself, several things must happen. First the reconnection of the DNA, which we have discussed earlier in this book. Next, all karma that holds us to the third dimensional, eye for an eye reality must be completed, resolved, and released. It takes the release of more than 50 percent of Earth karma for a person to achieve Earth Ascension. It also takes the release of whatever remaining other-planet karma that affects our lives and is connected with our karma on Earth. The next requirement is the healing of all core soul damage, which will automatically be done by the DNA reconnection and activation.

The final requirement is to clear our energy totally of all negative interference and all evil. We have done a great deal of this so far. If you have done the work of this book until now, you have cleared yourself of all or nearly all of the interference in your Earth incarnations. This means clearing and removing yourself from Earth negativity and the negative collective mass consciousness. It means clearing yourself of the negative emotions and attacks upon you by other people in this and other lifetimes, all forms of deliberate interference with your free will and life paths. It means clearing yourself of the negative dark from nonhuman sources. And it also means clearing your energy of all forms of negative interference originating from other planets or other-planetary negative Be-ings.

While most of the Universe is friend and mentor to Earth, and most of the Universe is made of Light, there are two notable exceptions. These two planetary groups are the sources of much negative Earth destiny, and their interference is the basis of all that is evil and wrong on this planet. Both groups come from the Orion star system; I call one group Orion and the other group the negative Greys. While we have had the most direct interaction with Orion, they are only half of the Source of All Evil on Earth, whereas the negative Greys are the other half. In my understanding, the negative Greys are renegades of a more positive culture, but the Orions are negative Be-ings from a totally negative planet.

The negative Greys are part of the Source of All Evil and are a manifestation of the Orions. The Greys are the Orions' allies and possibly their creations. I consider all evil on Earth to be a manifestation of the Source of All Evil, and every truly negative other-planet nasty I have dealt with seems to derive from Orion or the negative Greys. The Orions do the Greys' dirty work with a variety of electrical technologies designed to disrupt human life. The negative Greys are much less subtle, they want to destroy us and destroy the planet, and they work most of all to destroy all sources of the Light. The Orions do this as well. While the Light from beyond Earth has some defense from both of these groups, we on Earth—with our reduced DNA, damaged creation, and embattled and restricted awareness—are much more vulnerable. We have been taken over, and our planet taken over almost totally.

This is a pessimistic analysis, but it is coming to an end. Since the time of the 1987 Harmonic Convergence, tremendous outpourings of help have been channeled to this planet and to Earth people. We have been granted massive acceleration in our evolution: our Light vibrations have been raised and so has the planet's, for the purpose of throwing off—and throwing out—the negative aliens forever. We have been granted the reconnection of our DNA, and given the karmic dispensation and acceleration of working first with the Lords of Karma and now with Divine Director. Ascension is being offered to us in attainable ways for the first time since Orion destroyed Atlantis ten thousand years ago. We have achieved a tremendous increase in awareness on Earth in a very short time. When the negative Greys and Orion are removed from Earth, the Goddesses will walk here again. Even this is beginning to happen now.

Both Orion and the negative Greys can be defeated, and they are being removed from the Earth. Since the Earth is our planet,

Earth people are expected to make the requests to heal and defend it, and to participate in the process. It is our free will and it has to be our choice. This is a requirement of Karmic Law. We have not been given the awareness or the means to do these things until now. We presently have both the awareness and means. With the requests now being made through the Lords of Karma and Divine Director, the forces of the Light are permitted to do the work. We have only to ask. The catch has been that we were kept so totally in the negative dark that we had no idea what to ask for or even that asking was needed. Most people have long been aware that things are not right here, but few knew what was wrong, or why, or what to do.

It is my understanding that karma can only be healed in the body. We must incarnate on Earth to heal our Earth karma, and we will not begin incarnations on other planets until we complete our karma here. Though we have all had lifetimes, actually series of lifetimes on other planets, we did not begin to incarnate on Earth until we completed our incarnations on those planets. Karma cannot be healed in the between life state—it can only be completed and healed while in body. The reconnection of our DNA and the healing of soul damage can also only be achieved while in incarnation. Likewise, the ending of negative interference from all sources.

By the same token, only people in body can heal the karma of the Earth. This is our planet, subject to our free will. Just as we can heal our own karma by realizing what is needed and asking for it, we must do the same for the Earth. The Light will not interfere with our choices and free will and will not make our decisions for us. They can help us only if we ask. They have the means and the willingness, and far more knowledge and technical ability than we can imagine. But by Karmic Law that requires no violating or manipulating of anyone's self-determination, the

Light will help us only if we ask. We also must know what to ask for.

Until now it's been a Catch-22. We can have what we ask for if we know what it is we need. We have been kept from any knowledge of what is wrong, who can help us, how to ask to fix it, or how to fix it ourselves. We have had no idea that life on other planets and dimensions exists, or that most of those planets would protect us if we asked. We have had no idea that we need protecting or who our off-planet enemies are. The fact that we have been kept in the dark is no accident; we have been kept deliberately unaware by the negative dark, by Orion and the negative Greys who have a vested interest in keeping control of us and the Earth. The increase in our Light vibration is a gift from other planets and has enabled the reconnection of our DNA, the healing of our soul damage, and a general increase in our overall psychic abilities. With these gifts and the granting of help by the Lords of Karma and Divine Director, we are being given the ability to ask for help and to know what to ask for. And we must do so.

When we ask to clear and heal our personal karma, we are healing more than ourselves. I have discussed the concept of critical mass previously. When enough individuals heal, our healing also heals the Earth. We can now take it a step further. As each of us clears ourselves of negative interference, we clear the negative dark from the planet. Once we cleared ourselves of human and Earth negativity, we encountered negativity from nonhuman sources. Having now cleared all of these, we must next clear ourselves and the planet of the negative dark, the negative interference and evil that is coming to us and to the Earth from other planets. We finally have the ability to end all of these karmas and the help and the methods to do so.

We also have the protection. By the raising of our vibration we are beyond the reach of most negativity and we will now raise our vibration still higher. The way to do this is familiar. Go to the Lords of Karma and Divine Director now and request the raising of your vibration beyond the point where negative alien interference can reach or affect you. Do the complete Earth karmic release process, followed by the complete off-planet karmic process. Next, ask the Lords of Karma and Divine Director, as well as your Guardian Angel and all the forces of the Light, to provide you with the full protection you will need to clear yourself of the negative dark from Earth and all other planets. Use the wording I have given. These are two extremely important requests to make and they must be done before you go any further.

In this chapter, we will deal with interference from Orion and will leave the negative Greys for later. The processes above, however, are for protection from both groups. I realize that the information I am giving you is increasingly bizarre, but please bear with me. What you receive in your own meditation will give you the confirmation you need. Interference from Orion mostly consists of mechanisms that distort or disrupt your energy, create negative emotions, and prevent your full awareness. These appear most often as black boxes trailing coiled wires in your aura energy and chakras. I call them implants. The black boxes in turn are connected to an energy source or a beam from a small spaceship, and that spaceship is connected energetically or electrically to a larger one.

When we ask to remove these things, you will also see a variety of very small mechanisms in your chakras. These look something like radio transistors or computer chips, and like the black boxes, they are also implants. These occasionally manifest physically when they are removed. Implants are transmitters. They are other-dimensional, but electrical, and their presence in your Be-ing gives Orion electronic access to you. This access is for the purpose of indirect manipulation. They do things like create and amplify negative emotions. If your life has been shadowed by overwhelming fear or chronic difficulties with anger or depression, Orion implants could be the source. They also create defeatist attitudes that prevent your evolutionary growth. They keep you from your life path simply by keeping you too enervated to try.

The black boxes have another purpose. If you have ever seen swarms of snakes, spiders, squid, jellyfish, lizards, alligators, or other creepy-crawlies in your energy, they come from the black boxes. You can chase these around in your energy and never catch them, however, as they aren't really there. You spend time and energy fighting them, and they just move or come back. They are only pictures or holograms sent from the black box projectors. Their purpose is to create fear, and they do it quite well. They are also a smokescreen, a distraction, since the bugs can't hurt you but the boxes can. While you are chasing the spiders and calling for help to destroy them, the boxes are causing damage to your energy systems by disrupting the electrical processes of your mind and body. This damage is usually not serious in itself at this level and will be automatically healed, but enough of it results in harm. The consequences of this damage are more weakening of your will, your psychic abilities, and your core souls.

It seems that the higher your Light rises, the more Orion takes notice of you. The more they notice you, the more determined they are to stop your evolution. Your increase in Light is a threat to them, because those who achieve the awareness gain the ability to fight them and to remove their mechanisms. The implants and mechanisms are for the purpose of controlling

162

individual free will, keeping us from asserting ourselves against them and against their presence on Earth. They wish to control the Earth, but we are breaking their control. If your Light rises high enough to be of notice, the beams connecting the black boxes to the spaceships are used to create soul fragmentation in your energy. These are devastating energy attacks that cause significant damage and the shutting down of your psychic abilities for extended periods. The larger Orion spaceships also contain weapons. These shoot what look like warheads or bullets that then disperse like buckshot through your Mind Grid. The shrapnel causes mental damage, and the dozens of pieces are difficult to remove simply because of their great numbers.

I have been dealing with Orion for a number of years, and the relationship has not been pleasant. These Be-ings are not human and not to be considered life. They are a clear definition of evil, and it is fully ethical to destroy them. I have received a great deal of damage from all of the above horrors and have witnessed great damage to others. The requests for Orion's removal from the Earth, themselves and all their mechanisms, boxes, weapons, command centers, and spaceships, has already been made and granted. The war against them has now been won. I have cleared Orion implants from almost everyone I have done healing with in the last ten years. Now is the time to clear them from everyone, from all life on Earth, and that request has also been made to and granted by Divine Director and the forces of the Light. Orion is being expelled from Earth and all Earth Be-ings.

Though these requests have already been made and granted, and our other-planetary protectors and helpers have already ejected Orion from Earth and access to Earth, it is necessary to have as many people as possible to add their requests to mine. We are dealing with the concept of critical mass once again.

More than one person must ask, and the more who ask the better. I have also already asked for the protection of all people, all Be-ings, all life, and the planet, and those requests were granted, as well. We began with the requests for protection and will now do processes to clear your energy of all Orion implants, mechanisms, weapons, and their access to your energy. These things have already been deactivated in most people, but they must be removed.

A word about karmic contracts is in order here before we do the processes. As Be-ings living on a planet that has been at war since its creation, we all have karma from many lifetimes with the sources of evil on Earth. Orion and the negative Greys have effected us negatively, harmed us, damaged us, attacked us, manipulated us, and implanted us for thousands upon thousands of years. Orion was the cause of the explosion and destruction of Atlantis. They were involved in the Crusades, the Inquisition, the two World Wars, in the ongoing conflicts of the Middle East, and in fueling the hatreds of Bosnia, Rwanda, and dozens of other places.

Orion is the source of the network of negative energy portals that honeycomb the Earth. These are energy beams that channel disruption and interference to all the sensitive places on the planet—Israel and the Arab countries, India and Pakistan, Afghanistan, and all unstable nations. The smaller portals have more localized effects, even causing some homes to be centers of entity activity, rat and fire ant infestation, and other such nastiness. If you are being psychically attacked from whatever source, human or otherwise, Orion is probably fueling it or in some way involved. Their implants have taken over many weak or greedy people who are too willing to trade their Light for some form of power.

Everywhere there has been war and destruction on Earth, Orion has been involved. Their implants and weapon mechanisms reincarnate with us from lifetime to lifetime. In our many incarnations we have all met them again and again. We all have Earth karma with them, and since they are not Earth Be-ings we have other-planetary karma, as well. It is only with the addition of Divine Director to our karmic release processes that we can be cleared from Orion and it is now time to do so fully and forever.

This is exactly what we will do now. You have already requested protection and know that it is done. The primary protector against other-planet evil is Archangel Ashtar and his forces of the Light; he also works with Archangel Michael and the other archangels. Do not hesitate to call upon them in the work we are about to do. Because we are dealing with some heavy-duty nasties, I strongly suggest that the following work be done in a Cast Circle of Protection. Enter your meditation space, light candles and incense, and smudge the room and yourself with sage or cedar smoke before beginning. A purification bath with a cup of sea salt in the water, or salt rubbed on your chakras in the shower is also recommended after the ritual is completed.

To begin cast a Circle of Protection, asking that the Guardians of the Four Directions, plus the Center, Above and Below be with you. Ask for the Lords of Karma and Divine Director, Archangels Ashtar and Michael, your Guardian Angel, and the intergalactic forces of the Light. For Her protection, do not invite the Goddess into this ritual. Request that your circle be open to the Light but totally sealed against all evil. Now, ask to speak with the Lords of Karma and Divine Director and state the following:

I declare to the Universe and to the Light that I reject Orion and all their machinations and evils on Earth and on all other planets forever.

I declare to the Universe and to the Light that I reject Orion and all their evil, all their transistors, implants, boxes, weapons, beams, spaceships, command centers, and all their access to my energy through all the levels and components of my Be-ing, all dimensions, all connections, all systems, and between them, from Earth and all other planets through all lifetimes and between them forever.

I ask of the Lords of Karma, Divine Director, and the Light to end all my karma and all karmic contracts with Orion and all of the above, from Earth and all other planets through all lifetimes and between them forever.

I make formal declaration of total karmic severance from Orion through all incarnations, lifetimes, and between-life states on all planets forever.

I ask for these things on Earth and on all other planets and between them, through all lifetimes and between them, through all multidimensions and between them, of and between all dimensions of my multidimensional Be-ing.

I ask for these things
fully, completely, permanently, and forever,

Through all the levels and components of my Be-ing, all dimensions, all connections, all systems, and between them, through all lifetimes and between them, through all multidimensions and between them, of and between all dimensions of my multidimensional Be-ing.

I ask for these things
immediately and instantly,
past present and future,
NOW.

Wait for a response. You may or may not hear a yes, and you may even hear applause; no one will be refused. There will be immediate activity in your energy, and you may go on with the following while it continues. If you are given other instructions, of course follow them.

Now that you have cancelled your karmic contracts with Orion from Earth and all other planets, ask the Lords of Karma and Divine Director to remove from your energy through all the components, connections, levels, and systems of your Be-ing, all negative transistors, implants, boxes, weapons, beams, spaceships, command centers, all evil from all sources, and all their access to you forever. Ask that all of these evils and mechanisms be annihilated, extinguished, uncreated, and obliterated forever, along with all of their sources and perpetrators. Do the full off-planet karmic process; it is important and necessary.

Next, all in one process, ask the Lords of Karma and Divine Director to heal and regenerate you fully from all the damage of all the negatives above. Ask to purify your energy totally of all replication of these evils, and to replace any components or connections that are too damaged to heal easily or that were carrying replication of the mechanisms. Ask for full reconnection to the Light, and that all systems be brought back to optimal function and opening. Ask for absolute, complete, and total safety and protection forever. Continue and complete both the full Earth karmic process and the off-planet karmic process.

Finally, ask the Lords of Karma and Divine Director to seal your energy for the Light, and unto the Light and unto protection forever. It is extremely important to use this precise wording.

Do the full Earth karma and off-planet karmic processes to complete this. This last request will cause your Crown to be closed up for repatterning for about twenty-four hours. For some people it will take longer, and the closing will begin almost immediately. Wait until you are reopened to continue psychic work (other than the opening of your Circle). Though the closing is uncomfortable, it is necessary for the energy repairs and repatterning these requests have initiated. Making the above requests will provide you with a level of safety and protection you have not had before. The closing up will not interfere with any of your earthplane activities.

Thank the Lords of Karma and Divine Director, Archangels Michael and Ashtar, your Guardian Angel, and the intergalactic forces of the Light. Thank and release the Guardians of the Seven Directions (North, South, East, West, Center, Above and Below). Appreciate for a moment what you have been given. Open your Circle by stating: "This Circle is open but unbroken. Merry meet and merry part, and merry meet again. Blessed Be." A salt bath or sea salt rubbed on your chakras in the shower is recommended after the finish of this work.

During the ritual and your requests to the Lords of Karma and Divine Director, you may have been shown implants or mechanisms in your energy. Some of these were very far out in your soul structure energy, while others were quite close to the physical levels. Some of the mechanisms were located in chakras and others in your aura through layers of energy bodies. They may have been placed in your Tube of Light or your Crystal Shaft. Most of them existed on multiple levels of your energy anatomy, and most have reincarnated in your energy for multiple lifetimes. You may be shown images of some of these lifetimes. Unless you are told to do so, you will not need to ask for specific clearing for any of these lifetimes or mechanisms, as the wording of your request covers all of them. The images are mainly for your information. I have had many people treat my discussions of evil with scorn until they do the meditation and see these things for themselves. Some of what you see may be disturbing, but realize that you are only seeing it because it is leaving. The fact that it is gone is something to rejoice about.

It will take about three days for all implants and mechanisms to be fully cleared from your energy. You may see them or feel the activity of their release during this time. You may see angels moving through your energy to do the removal and destruction of the mechanisms. Welcome them and thank them. Angels seem to do this work with a wonderful, fierce glee; they delight in fighting this type of evil and it does not harm them. It will take about a week for the damage from the mechanisms to be healed. Again, you will perceive a great deal of activity in your energy systems. Welcome it.

Once this is done and your Crown is open again, if you are a civic-minded person, you might Cast a Circle once more to do a service for the planet. Repeat the ritual above, this time designating it for "the Earth, all Be-ings, and all life." Use that exact phrase. Do the same requests for the Earth instead of for yourself. A critical mass of people doing this will help clear and heal the planet of some very clear and present evil. Many people ask me about doing this healing for their loved ones. This is not something to do for others, as it is a karma they must choose and do for themselves. But in doing it for the Earth, all Be-ings, and all life, you are doing it for them, as well.

While I realize that the material of this chapter and the next contains some very scary stuff, please realize that through the work of this book you have come a very long way in protecting yourself from whatever may arise. When you began this work, you had no protection from Orion at all and from the implants already in your energy. You have carried this evil, we all have carried this evil, for many lifetimes and for many thousands of years. That you are seeing it now is because the distortions and our lack of awareness are being removed. The work you are doing does not create these things in your energy—it's already there. The work of this book has served to clear and protect you from a variety of very nasty stuff. I can only tell you what I tell people who see these things in healings: this is pain leaving, bless it, and let it go. Be grateful and thankful that its gone.

With each piece of nastiness that leaves your energy, your vibration and total Light increases. By this time, you are truly on the Ascension path. You are much brighter now than you have ever been before. Your real Light can now shine through to make you all that you can be. You have been prevented from being all that you can be until now. With these clearings, you will be aware of your growth and your rapid evolution. You will begin to be aware of what you have gained. And what the Earth has gained, as well.

11

THE SOURCE OF ALL EVIL

The other group of negative aliens we are dealing with on Earth have been here since the creation of the planet. They want to own this planet, and they want to own us. With their friends, the Orions—and the negative Greys, who come from very near the Orion star system—have made every effort to disable Earth and Earth people from all ability to access our higher potential. One of their agendas is to take over and take charge of Earth DNA. Our full complement DNA contains all the genetics of life on all the living planets of the Universe. Barbara Marciniak has named this "the living library." The Greys themselves have difficulty in reproducing their kind, and they want the power of controlling planetary diversity.

Psychics on Earth have known about the negative Greys for a long time. They are the caricature E.T. figure I have seen used as a joke in everything from comic books to bars of soap. There is E.T. jewelry with eyes that light up and E.T. beach towels. They appear as small rubbery-looking creatures with greyish-green skin, pear-shaped oversized heads, and oversized black almond-shaped eyes without pupils. When most people think of aliens, this is what they imagine. In fact, with only a few exceptions, most people from other planets look the same as us. (The

Pleiadians look like beautiful Earth people and we are descended from them.)

The Greys have difficulty in reproducing because of the pollution and destruction that the negative forces of their planet have caused. There are negative and positive Greys, and they are as much at war with each other as the negative Greys are at war with Earth. The negative Greys consist of about a quarter of their planet. Only 5 percent of their people are fertile, and they have sought the inhabited planets for genetic material they can use for their reproduction. Earth DNA, or some aspect of it as the living library, contains what they need. In the case of the positive Greys this has resulted in some friendly alliances with Earth people and people of other planets. In the case of the negative Greys it has resulted in abductions and terror.

I am aware of at least one psychic who has had a cooperative experience with the positive Greys. She has worked closely with a Grey scientist that can only be described as a Light-Being. She has willingly contributed her own eggs and allowed herself to incubate human-Grey eggs for Grey reproductions. When the fetuses reach a certain point of development they are taken from her body for completion and birth on Grey ships. She is aware of several children she has contributed to the positive Greys, and has met some of them on the psychic levels once they were grown. After more than a dozen such "pregnancies" over many years she decided that she didn't want to continue. Having the pregnancies taken from her was as emotionally wrenching as any Earth miscarriage. She still has contact and help from the scientist, and contact occasionally with her half-Grey offspring, who are instrumental in ending the reign of the negative Greys. The relationship and the woman's contributions to it were totally by her consent, and she has been treated with the utmost respect throughout. She considers her interactions with the positive Greys as "experiences," rather than abductions.

The woman's experience with Tion, the Grey scientist, began almost with her birth. Her first visit to Grey ships happened when she was six months old. The ships landed thereafter in a pond in her back yard and she was taken to them frequently. She felt that the Greys reminded her of who she was and what her purpose in life was. They validated her past life memories and experiences and taught her multidimensional travel; she met on the ships much-loved people who were members of her soul group. Tion helped her to remember her full potential and who she really is in the Universe. As a galactic warrior of the Light, he was and is her ambassador to the galaxy and her protector on Earth. In her current visits to the positive Grey ships, the woman serves as a teacher about Earth to the positive Greys who are acting as our protectors against the negative Greys and Orion.

Like Earth, the Greys' home planet was created with a positive vibration. Orion attacked the Greys' planet. They seeded it with negativity, as they have done on Earth, and the Greys' planet couldn't withstand the bombardment. The planet was taken over. The Orions have no emotions and scorn them, and they are fascinated with manipulating others' emotions to control people and countries. By Orion interference and electronics, the taken-over Greys lost their ability to have their own emotions. With the love removed there was nothing left. Some of the Greys were able to clear themselves of the negativity by vibrational frequency mechanisms. They wear a type of electronic badge for the purpose and have provided that technology to help Earth.

The Greys see energy visually and are technologically more advanced than Earth. Those able to overcome the Orion negativity were able to maintain their purity and emotions—they have a compassionate angelic quality. They have been fighting to regain the Light on their planet and repopulate it with Light DNA. The positive Greys have been fighting both the negative Greys and the Orions for thousands of years, since the creation of the Greys' planet was attacked by Orion. They have also aided Earth in removing both Orion and the negative Greys' attacks, spaceships, mechanisms, and energy from this planet. They are helping to prevent on Earth what happened to their home.

For a period of a few years I had experience with the positive Greys in a healing team I called "the Jupiter Surgical and Comedy Team." This group of strange-looking healers appeared in some of my hands-on Reiki sessions. They were dressed in surgical attire and seemed to be in what looked like an operating room, which was on one of their ships. I called them "The Jupiter Surgical and Comedy Team" because one of the Be-ings, named Blue, did a running stand-up comedy routine while the others did the work. I experienced in myself and witnessed in others some intensive healing by them, until one day they chose to go home with a woman they had done healing for, and they left me.

They used instruments of colored Light to scan the body, lasers to operate and remove tissue, and other Light beams and instruments for physical and energetic cleansing and purification. They had an extremely high technological understanding of human anatomy, and they informed me that our Earth medical methods are barbaric and archaic in how they treat dis-ease. I once watched them remove a woman's liver, clean it, and return it to its place. In one case, I watched them set and fuse a broken collar bone in a few minutes. The woman had broken it in a motorcycle accident, and it was not properly set. The bones were fused but not matched. The Jupiter Team moved the bones into place, set and fused them, and the results were quite evident on the physical plane. I was always glad and relieved when they showed up in a healing, and they were quite funny in their comedy act.

The negative Greys are not so funny nor are they so willing to help. They are known on Earth for their abductions of many people. Where the positive Greys have sought willing help for their reproductive difficulties, the negative Greys have simply taken what they wanted. They have left many people terrorized and traumatized by unwilling and violent visits to spaceships where sexual and genetic material was removed. Some people have had their memories blocked, but they have uncovered by hypnosis the explanation for their emotional trauma and nightmares, their fears of going to sleep, the screen memories, lost time periods, and memories of sexual experiments. Screen memories are an implanted picture or image that arises whenever the person tries to think about, analyze, or understand their abduction. The pictures have nothing to do with what happened, but the confusion they cause can be frightening. People abducted by the negative Greys were used in the way of laboratory animals. In a culture that refuses to accept life on other planets and is quick to brand the people who have been abducted as crazy, those who have been abducted are very isolated.

The negative Greys' abduction program is finally at an end, but abductions are only the tip of the iceberg. As Orion attacked and damaged the creation of the Greys' planet, so did Orion and the Greys taken over by them attack the creation of the Earth. The attempt, of course, was to do to Earth what was done to the Greys' home planet. They succeeded for too long, but thanks to the Lords of Karma, Divine Director, and the Light, the Earth has now been cleared. We have been in much the same situation as the positive Greys, but with far less awareness and with none of the technical ability to protect or help ourselves. We have been quarantined in the Universe until our decision was made to accept the take-over and be as evil as our attackers, and lose our ability to love, or to fight for our planet's self-determination and freedom.

A critical mass has been reached of people ready to fight. Since we are unable to do the fighting ourselves, we have been offered all the other-planetary help that we need. Our part and participation in it, however, is based on the requirement that we ask for the help we are receiving, and ask that Orion, the negative Greys, and all their interference be removed from the Earth forever.

In the vision I was shown of what happened to Earth, I first saw the golden sphere of Light that I was told was the planet's original creation. I saw Nada, our creation Goddess, in that sphere and part of it. Next I saw what looked like a black space-ship, missile, or torpedo targeting and flying into that Light, directly attacking Nada. From the force of the attack, I saw two objects separating and emerging from the golden sphere. One was Light and the other was negative and dark; one was Nada Herself, and the other was what I later named the Negative Form. Everything that was created from that time on was created in pairs of Light and negative dark. As Nada's creation of Light continued, each Be-ing's creation came with another aspect of the Negative Form.

Many on Earth today feel that all creation is meant to be dual, containing Light and dark, good and evil. This is not so. Earth and all Earth life was created in absolute purity and perfection, but that perfection was fouled and taken away from us. It was not meant to be this way. Everything created on Earth was created by and with the Light, and meant to be fully of the Light. Our birthright has been stolen from us. To multiply the wrongs, everything created is also carrying the damage of the Negative

Form put into us by the negative Greys. That negative dark replicates in our DNA and increases and incarnates with us through all of our lifetimes on all planets. Along with the Negative Form, our creation has been compromised to allow access to our energy by both Orion and the negative Greys.

Our DNA was disconnected down to only two strands, enough for physical existence but not enough to give us the means to protect, clear, or heal ourselves, to fight our attackers, or even to know about them. We carry the DNA of all life in the Universe, but have had no knowledge that we do. Nor do we know that its benefit has been taken away from us. It is this DNA that has made us desirable to the negative Greys and promoted their attack upon Earth. We were truly made hostages and slaves.

Nada first created the Goddesses and the Goddesses then created us; the same replication of evil happened to the Goddesses and to our creation from them. Their creation was damaged like ours, and the Goddesses sacrificed their own well-being to take on as much of the damage to protect us as they could. We owe them a debt and we owe them healing. It was Orion, the negative Greys and their Negative Form creations that caused the Goddess energy to be removed from the Earth. The Goddesses were being too damaged by the negativity, their purity too compromised to be able to remain here. Their leaving opened the way for the patriarchal takeover—it was more than patriarchal as we understand it—and resulted in the loss of the Divine Feminine and most of the Light to this planet. The course of civilization from then on was open to the predations of the negative dark. If you have any awareness of Earth history, or if you ever listen to the daily news, you must realize what has been done to us, and why we have little to be proud of.

The Negative Form carries both negative Grey and Orion energy, and it became an intrinsic part of everything created on and for the Earth. While most people truly hunger for the Light and have been able to resist the takeover of evil, some have been weak or greedy for power and allowed the negative dark full play. Orion mechanisms manipulate and destroy positive emotions, and their access to our energy to do so has wreaked havoc. The Greys are even less subtle. In their conquest of Earth DNA and Earth dominance their bent has been to separate people from the Light. They do this by destroying and blocking our energy connections to Goddess and to all sources of the Light. This interference is done energetically, with the use of weapons and mechanisms that disconnect and damage our psychic connections, the Galactic Cord that is our Light and Goddess channel, and of course our DNA. By preventing our vibrational evolution they literally keep us in the dark, ignorant, helpless, and isolated.

Again, the reconnection of our DNA is the means to our freedom and self-determination. By the reconnection, not only of twelve strands but of our full DNA complement, we are given back the ability to heal ourselves, to reject the negative dark from our energy and our lives, and to heal the damage that's been done to us. With the raising of our Light vibration through the DNA reconnection, we are given the power and the means to fight for our freedom. Most importantly and primarily, we are given the information of what has happened to us, and the will to say no, and we are demanding our reconnection to the Light and to the Goddess. With the return of our DNA, all the rest falls into place automatically.

All of these things have already been requested of the Lords of Karma and Divine Director and the requests have been granted: our reconnection to the Light, the restoration of our awareness and DNA, plus the obliteration of the Negative Form, Orion, and the negative Greys, and all their mechanisms and weapons. This has happened step by step, starting with the obliteration of the Negative Form. Once they were granted in July, 1999, the requests to end Grey and Orion interference brought about a nine-month intensification of intergalactic warfare that ended a war that's gone on for thousands of years. All forces of the Light from every corner of the Universe have been involved in this final effort to end the takeover of Earth. The wars are completed and won. All Earth life is being cleared and healed, and the Goddesses are being healed and returned to Earth. The Goddesses are the highest expression and form of our own Be-ings.

While the work is all but done, we again come to the requirement for critical mass, the request for as many people as possible to heal themselves and the Earth. We have done this throughout this book in our clearing from all types of negative interference. We did it with Orion and will do it now with the Negative Form and the Greys. I have used the term "the Source of All Evil" to designate specifically the Greys, but also to include Orion. I use the term "and all their creations and manifestations" to mean the Negative Form and everything else like it in the disruption of Earth life and creation. As with the work of the last chapter, you will work in the safety of a Cast Circle of Protection and Light. Give yourself more time than usual for this work, and ask not to be interrupted for any reason.

Go to your meditation space, light your candles and incense, smudge yourself with sage or cedar, and formally cast your protective Circle. Ask the Guardians of the Four Directions, plus the Center, Above and Below, your Guardian Angel, and the protecting Archangels Ashtar, Michael and Gabriel to be with you. Ask also for the presence of the Lords of Karma, and

Divine Director, and the Earth's Karmic Board. Request that your Circle be open fully to the Light, but totally sealed against all evil. As in the last ritual, for Her protection, do not bring your Goddess into this Circle as yet. Ask also for the help and protection of all the intergalactic forces of the Light. This will be a powerful Circle indeed.

Your first request to the Lords of Karma, Divine Director, and all the Light Be-ings present is to raise your energy vibration above and beyond the point where the Source of All Evil and all of its creations and manifestations can reach, interfere with, or harm you. This includes the negative Greys, Orion, the Negative Form, all their mechanisms, weapons, their access to your energy, and more. Do the full Earth and off-planet karmic processes. Next, ask the Lords of Karma and all the Light Be-ings present to provide you with the full protection you will need to clear yourself forever of these evils. Use the wording I have given and again do both karmic release processes.

If at any time in this ritual you feel threatened, do not hesitate to call upon your Guardian Angel and Archangels Ashtar, Michael and Gabriel for aid, or the intergalactic forces of the Light. They are our primary protectors from evil and the negative dark. The Karmic Board is there to witness these healings in the name of the Light and the Earth. They are Be-ings of great love and Nada is among them. Do not fear them. The Guardians of the Directions are aspects of our Oversouls; they are protection personified. Only the Light will enter this Circle; you are protected and fully safe.

Now, in the witness and agreement of the Lords of Karma, Divine Director, the Karmic Board, and all the Be-ings of the Light, state the following:

I declare to the Universe and to the Light that I reject the Source of All Evil and all its creations and manifestations,

Orion, the negative Greys and the Negative Form, and all their machinations and evils in my energy and life on Earth and on all other planets forever.

I declare to the Universe and to the Light that I reject the Source of All Evil and all its creations and manifestations, Orion, the negative Greys and the Negative Form, all their mechanisms, weapons, implants, interference and evil, and all their access to my energy through all the levels and components of my Be-ing, all dimensions, all connections, all systems and between them, on Earth and all other planets through all lifetimes and between them forever.

I ask of the Lords of Karma, Divine Director, the Karmic Board and the Light to end all my karma and all karmic contracts with the Source of All Evil and all its creations and manifestations, Orion, the negative Greys, the Negative Form, all of their access to my energy and all of the above, from Earth and all other planets through all lifetimes and between them forever.

I make formal declaration of total karmic severance from the Source of All Evil and all its creations and manifestations, Orion, the negative Greys, the Negative Form through all incarnations, lifetimes and between-life states on all planets forever.

I ask for these things on Earth and on all other planets and between them, through all lifetimes and between them, through all multidimensions and between them, of and between all dimensions of my multidimensional Be-ing.

I ask for these things
fully, completely, permanently, and forever,

*Through all the levels and components of my Be-ing, all
dimensions, all connections, all systems and between them,
through all lifetimes and between them, through all multidimensions and between them, of and between all dimensions of
my multidimensional Be-ing.*

*I ask for these things
immediately and instantly,
past present and future,
NOW.*

Wait for a response. No one will be refused. If you are given
further instructions, follow them. Be sure to say thank you.
Then continue.

With all your karma and karmic contracts with these evils
cancelled, ask to annihilate, extinguish, uncreate, and obliterate
from your energy through all the components, levels, and systems of your Be-ing and between them, all evil, negative interference, mechanisms and access by them to your energy from
the Source of All Evil and all its creations and manifestations,
including Orion, the negative Greys and the Negative Form,
and all of their kind forever. Ask that all of these evils and their
perpetrators be annihilated, extinguished, uncreated, and obliterated at their sources. Do the full Earth and off-planet karmic
release processes to complete your request; it is important and
necessary to do this. If you are given further instructions or are
told there is something more to clear, do so.

Some explanation may be necessary here about the terms
"annihilate, extinguish, uncreate, and obliterate." They sound
bloodthirsty, but I assure you I am not a bloodthirsty person.
We are dealing here with the ending of evil, and it must be
ended in an unequivocal way, with no possibility of it returning
to do more harm. We are not asking to kill anything or to harm

anything or anyone that is alive or of life. We are asking to end our own destruction, and anything less than a total ending of these evils is not enough. We are doing these processes to protect life and all that is Light within us.

Next, all in one process, ask the Lords of Karma, Divine Director, the Karmic Board, and the Light to heal and regenerate you fully from all the damage from all the negatives above. Ask to purify your energy totally of all replication of these evils and their access to you, and to replace any components or connections that are too damaged to easily heal or that were carrying replication of alien or Earthly evil. Ask for full reconnection with the Light and full development of your Galactic Cord system. Ask that all systems be brought back to optimal function and opening. Ask for absolute, complete, and total safety and protection from the Source of all Evil and all its creations and manifestations, from Orion, the negative Greys, the Negative Form, and more forever. Continue and complete both the full Earth and off-planet karmic processes.

With another full request, ask the Lords of Karma, Divine Director, the Karmic Board, and the Light for total healing of your creation from all damage and interference by the Source of All Evil and all its creations and manifestations, including Orion, the negative Greys, and the Negative Form. Request complete and total healing and regeneration, total purification from evil and return to purity, replacement of any components or connections that cannot be easily healed, or that were carrying replication of evil. Ask to return your creation and all systems to optimal function and opening, and absolute, complete, and total protection and safety forever. Use the above wording, and do the Earth and off-planet karmic processes to complete your request. You may now repeat this process for your Goddess, whether you know Her name or not, and She may be safely invited to join the Circle at this time.

Finally, make the following request, using the exact wording below. Ask the Lords of Karma, Divine Director, the Karmic Board, and the Light to seal your energy against the Source of All Evil and all its creations and manifestations, including Orion, the negative Greys, and the Negative Form forever. Ask to seal your energy forever against all attacks, all intergalactic, inter-planetary and intra-planetary warfare, all conquest by evil forces, all damage and harm by evil of all types, all access by evil, all negative interference, all negative programming and mechanisms, all prevention and blockage of your evolution and Ascension, all obstruction and prevention of the evolution of the Earth, all life and all Be-ings. Complete this with the Earth and off-planet karmic processes. You may repeat this for your Goddess, as well. Again, no one will be refused, but you may be given further instructions.

Thank the Lords of Karma, Divine Director, the Karmic Board, your Guardian Angel, Archangels Ashtar, Michael and Gabriel, and the intergalactic forces of the Light. Thank your Goddess, and thank and release the Guardians of the Directions (North, South, East, West, the Center, Above, and Below). Take a moment to understand and appreciate what you have been given in this ritual. Make the formal Circle opening statement, "This Circle is open but unbroken. Merry meet and merry part, and merry meet again. Blessed Be." It is best to take a salt bath, using a cup of sea salt in your bath water, or rub sea salt on your chakras in the shower after completing this work. You have dealt with and released a great deal of strong negativity, and though the negativity is on deeper levels than the physical application of salt can reach, it is a good thing to do.

As with your similar request for energy sealing in the last chapter, your Crown will be closed for repatterning for about twenty-four hours. Wait until you are open again to do further karmic or psychic work, other than the opening of your Circle. A lot of healing will be accomplished in your energy while your Crown is closed and some major protections will be installed. The total healing requires about a month. You will feel yourself being worked on during this time and will probably experience other periods of your Crown being closed. Having declared yourself so fully for the Light, the Light will protect and heal you. You have fulfilled the karmic requirement of participating in your healing and in the healing of the Earth by making these requests that ask for help. By doing so, you have greatly increased your own evolution and that of the planet, and added to the critical mass that will clear and heal the Earth of all evil forever.

You have also asked for these healings for your Goddess. Each of us has a series of Energy Selves (see *Essential Energy Balancing*) and a Goddess that exists beyond your Oversoul. Everyone has a Goddess. If you do not know Her name, just ask for the healing of "your Goddess" and it is enough. Her name will probably be given to you in the ritual; She will be someone you have always known. The Goddesses were created for Earth by Nada, Earth's Great Mother creation Goddess. They were harmed in their creation as we were, and have been prevented from their work on Earth and from their work with us. We must heal them as we heal ourselves. (There will be much more on this in *Healing the Goddess*, and the work of healing the Goddesses is now being done.) By asking to heal your Goddess you are asking to heal the highest vibrational expression of your Be-ing, as well as healing your evolution, and the evolution and Ascension of the planet. If you have not been aware of Goddess energy, or known your Goddess until this time, you are also in for a pleasant surprise when you ask to meet and heal Her.

Once you have completed this work and your energy is opened again, you may wish to repeat the above processes for the Earth Herself. Again, this work has already been done, but in the concept of critical mass it is still needed. Cast your Circle of Protection once more and repeat your requests, designating them for "the Earth, all life, and all Be-ings." In doing this, you are helping to heal all people, all the animals and plants, and all that lives. Because of the intensity of the ritual you have just done, it is probably best to do the Earth healing on another night.

With the influence of the negative Greys, Orion, and the Negative Form ended on Earth, a great deal of the destruction, wars, and wrongs that increasingly mark this planet will end. A great amount of suffering will be lifted from all people. In healing yourself, you will find that all the things that have been stuck in your life and your energy will clear. Your path will be smoother in every way. You will have the satisfaction of knowing that you have taken your power and your birthright, and you will have a new and greater understanding of who you are. You have made the effort to increase your Light and the level of Light on the planet. Perhaps as more and more of us do this, we will hear the difference on the daily news. Instead of disasters there will be peace accords and healing breakthroughs. The world will change for the better. Understand and know that you have had a part in this change. Be aware and be proud.

12
CONCLUSION

There is one final process to complete the work of *Reliance on the Light* and it's a very special one. At Womongathering, 1999 I was energy attacked so badly by the negative Greys that I despaired of surviving the weekend. To add to the misery, the attack was channeled through someone I'd thought of as a friend. My Galactic Cord was cut, chakras on each of several levels were negatively sealed, a number of energy channels were negatively rerouted and short-circuited, and several blockages and obstructions were placed in my energy. There was major damage to many connections, chakras, and levels in addition. All of my psychic abilities were totally stopped and I had no access to the Lords of Karma or to any other help. Even my pendulums didn't work. The effect of the Galactic Cord being severed, once it has developed fully, is total enervation, nonstop crying, and absolutely wanting to die. On top of all this, I had workshops to teach through the weekend, and a number of women attending had experienced attacks as well.

Three women attempted to help me, spending the evening in my cabin, talking and trying to calm me down. No one really knew what to do and I couldn't tell them. One made a suggestion, however, that began the process of my healing, offered the means for the healing of future attacks, and gave me a measure of hope. I took her suggestion, used it, and later developed it into a full process. Her suggestion was to ask for Archangel Michael's Sword of Protection and his Chalice of Regeneration and Healing. I made the request to the Lords of Karma (I was a week or so short of first meeting Divine Director) and the healing began.

Nearly a year later with the help of another healer I discovered the Karmic Shield. This is the protection that prevents karma once completed from returning. Apparently I had incarnated without it. I asked for the Shield as well, and the process felt complete for the first time. The three tools—for lack of a better term—had also been King Arthur's Sword Excalibur, his magick scabbard (the Shield), and the Holy Grail. They have proved life saving to me and important for everyone who has them. Since discovering these items I have requested them for everyone in all of my workshops.

The Sword, Chalice, and Shield have been given freely by the Lords of Karma, Divine Director, and Archangel Michael to everyone who has made the request. They are a part of *Healing the Goddess*. I did not expect to offer them in this book, but a number of processes here have crossed into the Energy Balancing II methods. This book on protection became more advanced than I expected it to be when I started it. As its conclusion and a great gift from Archangel Michael, I am permitted to bring the Sword, Chalice, and Shield to everyone here. If you have gone through all the processes of this book, you deserve them!

This is a simple Lords of Karma and Divine Director process—it does not require the casting of a Circle. It is best done the last thing at night before sleep and it can be done in bed. You will feel movement in your energy from the installation all night. In the morning, ask again if the Sword, Chalice, and

Shield are fully installed and if they are activated. If they are not, repeat the request. It is best to check occasionally to see if all three remain activated. For some reason fluctuations or overloads in your energy can take one or more of them off line. Requests are made for full insulation to prevent this, but it's wise to check just the same.

These protections come with a responsibility. I have spent years of having my energy attacked, of asking and pleading for help and protection, and for healing of the damage. At the time that the Sword was granted to me, it came with almost an order from Archangel Michael. I was told that it was time to pick up the Sword, time to fight to protect the Goddess and the Light. This was a foreign idea to me. I asked how I was to do that—I'm no warrior. (My friends joke that I'm not allowed to handle sharp objects—or to drive or cook.) I asked for Michael's guidance and help in knowing when and how to use His Sword. The next time I needed it, the Sword was there. I picked it up and fought the negative Greys. I cannot begin to tell you how good, how totally empowering, it felt to do it.

In this process, you will request each of the protections and ask where they will be installed in your energy. They will be installed in different places for different people. If you do not perceive where they are to be placed, but you are not refused them, they will be installed in your energy just the same. You may learn where they are later, but it's not terribly important that you know. It's only important that they are there. One woman who has the tools tells me that they seem to move around in her energy. You are considered eligible to receive them if you have dedicated yourself to the Light. The process follows.

Archangel Michael's Sword, Chalice, and Shield

• Ask to speak with the Lords of Karma, Divine Director, and Archangel Michael.

• Ask if you may have Archangel Michael's Sword of Truth and Protection installed in your energy. Its use is to fight evil.

• If the answer is yes, ask where the Sword is to be installed in your energy.

• When you know, do a complete Lords of Karma and Divine Director Earth process requesting that the Sword of Archangel Michael be installed in your energy at the designated location on all levels and through all systems. It's time to pick up the Sword to protect life on Earth—ask for the ability and safety to do so.

• Next ask if you may have Archangel Michael's Karmic Shield installed in your energy. It protects you from the return of old karma.

• If the answer is yes, ask where the Shield is to be installed.

• Do a complete Lords of Karma and Divine Director Earth process requesting that Archangel Michael's Karmic Shield be installed in your energy at the designated location on all levels and through all systems.

• When this is done, ask if you may have Archangel Michael's Chalice of Healing and Regeneration installed in your energy. Its use is for automatic energy healing.

• If the answer is yes, ask where the Chalice is to be installed.

• When you know, do a complete Lords of Karma and Divine Director Earth process requesting that the Chalice of

Archangel Michael be installed in your energy at the designated location on all levels and through all systems.

• Next, ask the Lords of Karma, Divine Director, and Archangel Michael to fully activate the Sword, Shield, and Chalice immediately, continuously, irrevocably, and forever in your energy, through all the levels, components, and systems of your Be-ing and between them. Ask for full insulation of your energy to protect the activations.

• Clearly see yourself picking up the Sword. Ask for Archangel Michael's guidance as to when to do so and how to use it, and ask for his protection. Agree to use this Sword only to protect and defend the Light and the Goddess.

• Do both the full Earth karmic process and the off-planet karmic process to finish.

• Thank the Lords of Karma, Divine Director, and Archangel Michael, and know that it is done and that you are safe.

These protections have already been installed in the Earth, the Earth planetary grids, and in the Solar System. In the interest of critical mass, you may ask for them again for the planet. With this final process and the safety that they offer, you have come a long way in the healing and protection of yourself, of the Goddess, of all life, and of the Earth. The work of this book is now complete. I can only wish for you everything this book has already given you. It offers you much more than you know or can understand at this time.

Diane Stein
Full Moon in Virgo
March 19, 2000

www.crossingpress.com

BROWSE through the Crossing Press Web site for information on upcoming titles, new releases, and backlist books including brief summaries, excerpts, author information, reviews, and more.

SHOP our store for all of our books and, coming soon, unusual, interesting, and hard-to-find sideline items related to Crossing's best-selling books!

READ informative articles by Crossing Press authors on all of our major topics of interest.

SIGN UP for our e-mail newsletter to receive late-breaking developments and special promotions from The Crossing Press.

WATCH for a new look coming soon to the Crossing Press Web site!